A A K Graham
March 195?

THE
CHURCH
AND THE
SOCIAL
ORDER

*'We have this treasure
in earthen vessels.'*
II Corinthians, iv, 7.

THE CHURCH AND THE SOCIAL ORDER

A Historical Sketch

S. L. GREENSLADE, M.A.

*Canon of Durham and
Lightfoot Professor of
Divinity in the
University of
Durham*

SCM PRESS LTD
56 BLOOMSBURY STREET, LONDON W.C.1

First published November 1948

Distributed in Canada by our exclusive agents
The Macmillan Company of Canada Limited
70 Bond Street, Toronto

Printed in Great Britain by
Northumberland Press Ltd.
Gateshead on Tyne

Contents

Preface

IT is easier to say what this book is not than what it is. It is not a history of Christian ethical or sociological theory. It is not a survey of the whole impact of Christianity upon civilization. It is largely confined to political, economic and, in a much restricted sense, social life. It says little of the steady permeation of society by Christian ideas, or of the work of individual Christians, or of those rebellious prophets and reformers, like Robert Owen or Karl Marx, whose thought and work would have been impossible without their Christian background. It is an attempt to map out the lines of an answer to the question, What has the Church done? Those who put the question commonly mean, What have the clergy done in social life, or what has been effected by Christian movements so organized that they can be counted more or less official? Although this is a wrong notion of the Church and of the way Christianity ' works ' in society, I have accepted this limitation, allowing myself only occasional exceptions.

Even with this restriction, the ground to be covered is enormous. Partly because of the predetermined size of the book and partly because of ignorance, I have had to select. The form adopted is pyramidal. The base, in Chapter I, is the whole Church; in Chapter II there begins a geographical limitation to Western Europe, continued in Chapter III and further reduced to Protestant Churches in Chapter IV and to England in Chapter V.

There are some large books on this subject, or parts of it, which will supply further detail. As they tend to be storehouses of material, I have tried, not very successfully, to make a *story* out of the limited amount this book will hold. No bibliography has been included since the books which will best assist further study have been mentioned in footnotes, with the exception of J. N. Figgis: *From Gerson to Grotius* (C.U.P., 1907), which is particularly valuable for Chapter IV.

Finally, this is not a balanced judgement upon the Church. I know the case against it, especially in that official character which is my main theme; and I have frequently alluded to what it was not my business to describe. But it is not the Christian who is surprised at sin, within or without the Church. There is something pathetic in the rationalist who blames Christians for those imperfections which he believes will vanish with religion.

S.L.G.

The College, Durham.
March, 1948.

The Early Church

'PEOPLE knows well enough what's good for them to do
and what isn't without being dictated to by a clergyman,' said Mrs. Brattle of Startup Farm to the Vicar of
Bullhampton; and miller Brattle held similar views, for he
described Parson Smallbones as 'a good man as didn't go
meddling with folk'. Not that this opinion was a peculiarity
of the Brattle family. At Loring, old Parson Marrable ' was a
good sort of man in his way', the waiter thought, 'but not
much of a preacher. The people liked him because he never
interfered with them.' To turn from Trollope to history, Lord
Melbourne had a sincere respect for the Church of England
as an institution. ' It was,' he often said, ' the best church, the
least meddling.' Even so high-minded and religious a man as
Sir Walter Scott disliked the enthusiasm which makes ' religion
a motive and a pretext for particular lines of thinking in
politics and in temporal affairs '.

On the other hand the cry goes up, ' Why doesn't the Church
do something about it? ' In 1914 and in 1939 there were
many who asked, ' Why doesn't the Pope do something about
it? ' And even if the Church is not saddled with the whole
blame for every social ill—for war, hunger and unemployment,
slavery, slums and sweating—at least, it is said, the Church
could have done more about them.

Logically these different attitudes rest upon different beliefs
about religion or about the function of the Church and its
authorities. With an inconsistency not unknown to the rationalist, unbelievers may belabour the Church with both cudgels
at once.[1] More sympathetic critics will perceive that the
problem springs from the very nature of Christianity, which
is neither wholly other-worldly (as some oriental religions have

aspired to be) nor wholly concerned with this world. It cannot accept social utility as the sole or supreme test of its success, nor can it disclaim social duties as if its endeavours were merely to purge the soul from worldly desires.

The Christian Dilemma

This dilemma or tension was present in the teaching of Jesus Himself. It had been less apparent in the religion of Israel since, on the whole, the Hebrews had a high regard for the natural gifts of God, the Creator of all things, and since their moral standards, however lofty, were not conceived in terms of renunciation. The will, not matter, was the seat of evil. Socially, too, their greatest prophets taught them how much of their duty to God lay in duties towards their neighbours. God demands righteousness. Moreover, for most of the period covered by the Old Testament, they had no belief in a future life and therefore no idea of a purpose of God which cannot be fulfilled in this world. Not only must their duty to God be performed here and now, in a community accepting God as its King, but also God Himself, when He chooses to bring in the Day of the Lord, must manifest His power and love, must vindicate His righteousness, in this world. The perfect society must one day come—on earth.

It is true that this outlook had been modified in the three or four centuries immediately before the days of Jesus Christ, centuries of contact with Persian dualism and Greek specula- tion (both of them disparaging the flesh), centuries during which a growing faith in immortality began to turn men's thoughts away from any final satisfaction in this world. Still, the essential moral outlook of the Old Testament had been formed before this happened. The good Jew, hugging his belief that righteousness is rewarded in this life, could hardly object if the value and success of his religion were measured by the righteousness of Israel, the chosen people of God.

Although it would be an exaggeration to deny any other- worldliness to the Old Testament, the growth of this spirit is great and rapid in the New. Jesus did not release the Christian from a single social obligation. He came to fulfil the Law, not to destroy it. He even, to the dismay of some moralists, went on talking about rewards for good conduct. Yet the spirit had changed. 'My kingdom is not of this world.' History indeed matters, for God acts, and by acting reveals Himself, in history; and in Jesus Christ God incarnate lived in history. But the goal and explanation of history lie beyond itself and not in the distant historical event of a perfect society in this world. So, too, the worth of each individual who enters into the stream of history is not to be measured simply by his contribution towards ' a better world '. What he is worth to God, only God knows; it can be revealed only in the life beyond history which is his destiny. People matter for what they will ultimately be.

The problem of the Christian Church has always been how to keep faith with both sides of her Lord's teaching, how to combine the social duties which she acknowledges with her pastoral mission of preparing men for heaven by keeping before them the paramount importance of the world beyond history. In principle the problem may be soluble just in so far as God prepares us by duties in this world for a destiny beyond it, but the application of the principle is never simple. Men tend to extremes, sometimes of cloistered piety, sometimes of absorption in business, the balance is hard to strike, and always there are sin and ignorance to reckon with. A surge of optimism may lead Christians to concentrate on social improvement, justified by the law of love; hostility to religion may drive the Church to erect barriers between herself and the world, justified by her duty to nourish the souls of the faithful and to renew her own vitality. Within the Church, also, there will be differences of emphasis. Tension is inescapable and probably it is very stimulating. If the success of the Church is to be measured at all, it must be in the light of all her functions. If she is to be known by her fruits, then part of the fruit must be her influence upon society. But visible social progress cannot be the only measure of a Church which is charged with the care of immortal souls.

The New Testament

'And all that believed were together, and had all things common; and they sold their possessions and goods, and parted them to all, according as any man had need.' (Acts ii, 44-45.)

This first episode in the social history of the Christian Church is instructive. That love of the brethren should manifest itself in material aid is not peculiar to Christianity, but there is here an unusual blend of social responsibility and irresponsibility not always perceived by those who talk of early Christian communism. To sell capital assets and exhaust the proceeds was not an action based on social theory. It was possible only for men who had no such theory, who felt no responsibility for society as that would be understood to-day, precisely because they expected the speedy return of the Lord accompanied by the transformation or the end of this world. Spontaneous charity and other-worldliness in one form or another were to shape the social activity of the early Church; and however necessary a more constructive sociology, they must always find place in authentically Christian practice.

St. Paul, a missionary statesman no less than a theologian, had to grapple with these problems. He, too, knew the hope of a speedy Second Coming, and there were times when his experience of this present world suggested that separation from it alone could safeguard the purity of his converts. 'What communion hath light with darkness? And what concord hath Christ with Belial? Or what portion hath a believer with an unbeliever? . . . Come out from among them, and be ye separate, saith the Lord, And touch no unclean thing; And I will receive you.' (II Cor. vi, 14-17.) Further, where Jesus had been content to assume the actual sinfulness of all men ('if ye, being evil . . .'), St. Paul propounded a theory of the Fall and spoke of the weakness and sinfulness of the flesh. 'In me, that is in my flesh, dwelleth no good thing.' (Rom. vii, 18.) He talked of buffeting his body (I Cor. ix, 27). He set celibacy above marriage. Now St. Paul certainly did not teach a formal dualism of evil matter and good mind or spirit. Flesh to him means our whole human nature in its fallen weakness. But separation from the world, ascetic discipline, at least one ascetic ideal (virginity) and the spirit-flesh antithesis, all to play a big part in the Christianity of the future, could find proof texts and something more in his writings.

On the other hand, while it is fundamental to St. Paul that our citizenship is in heaven, he does not disparage earthly citizenship. Following the Lord's 'Render unto Caesar the things that are Caesar's', he insists on the elementary civic duties (Rom. xiii). No belief in the immediate return of the Messiah is to justify laziness (I Thess. iv, 11; II Thess. iii, 10). Slaves are to serve their masters as under the eyes of God (Col. iii, 22). The fabric of government is itself a divine institution and social life the opportunity for Christian service. His loftiest and toughest passages of theology are commonly followed by moral application. Not that the Christian's *motive* will be the re-ordering of society. Paul's aim, arising from his ultimate other-worldliness, is missionary, that Greek and Jew, barbarian, Scythian, bondman, freeman, may become new creatures in Christ and inheritors of a heavenly kingdom. But as a result, transformed lives will transform society, while moral witness will assist the Gospel. I Peter takes the same line, echoing the words of Jesus. No more than sojourners and pilgrims on earth, we are nevertheless to have our 'behaviour seemly among the Gentiles that . . . they may by your good works which they behold, glorify God in the day of visitation.' Therefore, 'Honour all men. Love the brotherhood. Fear God. Honour the king.' (I Peter ii, 12-13, cf. Matt. v, 16; I Peter ii, 17.)

It may fairly be claimed that this missionary motive dominates the New Testament, other-worldly in its goal, but involving the moral transformation of society in that the Christian (so far as he is a Christian) accepts the law of love and becomes the channel of that divine love which is shed abroad in our hearts by the Holy Spirit, love not measured out piti-

lessly in response to each man's desert, but flowing generously
to meet his need. If in time, when the position of the Church
in the world has changed, the new spirit will lead to new
theories of society, yet essentially the Christian contribution to
social thought is its union of other-worldliness with an overwhelming emphasis upon love.

Before we leave the New Testament, some points of importance may be noted more briefly. First, there is one book,
Revelation, which exhibits so violent a hatred of the impious
and persecuting State that, taken alone, it could breed anti-
social ideas. Secondly, there is in the Epistle to the Hebrews
and in the Gospel and First Epistle of St. John a strain of
'Platonism' which can lead to a particular form of other-
worldliness, not specifically Christian but often attractive to the
Christian mind. It is not simply their moral dualism—'the
whole world lieth in the evil one'—with its sharpening of the
distinction between church and world, but the inclination to
assimilate the difference between good and evil to the difference between spirit and flesh, between the eternal-spiritual and
the temporal-material. Within the New Testament, indeed
within the books just mentioned, this tendency is checked
by a strong doctrine of Incarnation. The Word became flesh,
came to save the whole world. Later, however, this element
has frequently been used to sponsor that thorough-going
world-renunciation which regards the common concerns of
human society as chains upon the spirit, if not evil in themselves.

Finally, to return to the Lord Himself, no Christian can
escape the demand, 'Take up thy cross.' Jesus did not teach
asceticism as such, though he knew the value of bodily discipline. He did not scorn the simple pleasures of the world,
though he feared the demoralization of riches. He did not
seek suffering for its own sake; He accepted what was necessary to fulfil His own mission and He expected His followers
to do likewise. There can be no perfect society of evil men,
and there is no guarantee that men will ever cease to be evil
in this world. In one sense the law of love will provoke Chris-

tians to attempt the elimination of suffering; in another sense, love itself will cause Christians to suffer. We cannot make the removal of suffering as such our social aim, much less the removal of discomforts. Nothing so negative will do. It may be that throughout history to come, the *conquest* of suffering will be a totally different thing from its elimination.

Christianity and Paganism

For nearly three centuries the Church was not in a position to influence society through pressure upon the administration, local or central. Nor did it think much about influencing society, except indirectly through the better conduct of individual converts. Besides worship, the first duty of the Church was to grow, without compromising its own faith and moral demands. Confronted by a pagan society, lacking social prestige, unrecognized and frequently persecuted by secular authority, the Church was bound to distinguish itself sharply from the world. Conversion meant renunciation.

Pagan ideas about Christianity make this clear. Tacitus knew that the real objection to Christians was not the burning of Rome, but hatred of the human race, that is, either the prejudice which most men had conceived against them or (more probably) their apparent unsociability and ' superiority '. Although the humane Pliny who, as Governor of Bithynia, had to investigate complaints against Christians, reported to Trajan that they assembled for no evil purpose, but pledged themselves not to commit theft or adultery, not to break their word and not to deny a deposit, the common folk (and even educated men like Fronto, the tutor of Marcus Aurelius) circulated rumours of incest, infanticide and cannibalism. These misunderstandings of sacramental language were cleared up in time, so that Christian apologists of the second century appealed confidently to pagan knowledge of the Christian virtues. Much more serious was the charge that Christians were, if not seditious at any rate, useless citizens. So Celsus argued in the forceful attack which he delivered about the middle of the second century. The proportions of one of the ablest defences, Tertullian's *Apology* of A.D. 197, show that, while he could wellnigh ignore and easily retort charges concerning private morals, he was eager to establish the utility of Christian citizenship.

The difficulty and complexity of the Christian position may be illustrated from three writers. Some time in the second half of the second century, an unknown author composed an *Epistle to Diognetus*. ' Christians ', he writes, ' are not distinguished from the rest of mankind by locality or speech or customs.' *But* ' they dwell in their own countries, but only as sojourners; they take their share in everything as citizens, and they endure all hardships as strangers. Every foreign country is a fatherland to them, and every fatherland is foreign. . . . Their existence is on earth, but their citizenship is in heaven.' Having spoken of persecution, he continues, ' What the soul is in a body, this Christians are in the world. . . . They are kept in the world as in a prison-house, yet they themselves hold the world together.'

Is this visionary? Or is it true that only by other-worldliness can this world be transformed? The principles which this unknown writer set out so attractively had to be worked out concretely as the Church grew in strength.

At the turn of the second and third centuries, Tertullian, a Roman lawyer who had become a priest of Carthage, tried to accomplish this task. One group of his writings, pre-eminent among them the great *Apology*, is addressed to the pagan world, more particularly to Roman magistrates. Here Tertullian states what was quite true in fact, that Christians are not ' exiles from life ', that they share in all the business of the world, its arts and crafts, its commerce and industry, agriculture, law, military service. They have the common needs of mankind, they earn their living in ordinary ways. How they can be ' unfruitful in business ' he cannot understand. And more, they are honest in business and in their civic duties. They pay their taxes without cheating! They cannot worship the Emperor, but they loyally pray for him.

A fair argument, strongly pressed by other apologists. But how uneasy Tertullian was can be seen from the writings which he addressed to Christians. Afraid of contamination by daily contact with pagans, he warns them to withdraw as much as possible from society. So in *The Shows* he argues that Christians cannot attend the shows, the theatre, circus and arena, not so much because they may be immoral in content (for he expressly includes athletic contests) as because they are linked with idolatry. In his *The Crown*, he argues similarly against military service, not only because it involves killing, but because it will also entail attendance at idolatrous ceremonies. Another work, which he called *On Idolatry*, might to-day be entitled *The Church and the World*. Here he warns Christians off every activity remotely implicated in idolatry. Public service, military or municipal, is impossible since acknowledgement of some pagan cult will be demanded sooner or later. Thus a Christian cannot be a magistrate or a schoolmaster. Craftsmen must take care that the products of their industry will not be used as adjuncts to idolatry. The high gains of making costly cult-objects must be foregone. If pressed, his severe logic might seem to close one useful occupation after another, until he himself anticipates the objection, 'Who can take all these precautions? We shall have to go out of the world.' Well, he replies, that is better than staying in it as an idolater. In the last resort, the Christian must be prepared to die rather than compromise.

In detail Tertullian's position is impossible; adopted, it would have justified contemporary suspicion of Christianity as inherently anti-social, at least in anything but a perfect world. Yet one must admire his perception that its power lay in its absolute demands, its complete break with paganism. He did not wish to abandon the world to its sin, but to convert it by exhibiting, unblurred, the difference between light and darkness; and (it was he who said it) the blood of the martyrs would be the seed of the Church. In the end Tertullian's rigorism drove him to join the Montanist sect, the first example of those Puritan movements (though it had less

B

admirable characteristics as well) which have from time to time challenged the worldliness of the Church. The lawfulness and limits of compromise are always a problem to a missionary body.

With Tertullian we may contrast his elder contemporary, Clement of Alexandria, who stands, with many limitations, within the liberal and humanist tradition. First, unlike Tertullian, whose conception of Christianity as essentially revelation, led him to distrust human wisdom, Clement accepted philosophy as itself a gift from God, valuable both as a preparation for the Christian religion and an aid to its theology. If he and his greater successor Origen were perhaps a little too eager to 'keep abreast with modern thought', at least they made contact with thinkers of their day and sufficiently 'spoiled the Egyptians' to show up the weakness of pagan solutions to the riddle of the universe.

Next, Clement showed an interest in some particular social problems. In general, early Christians feared riches and were far from developing any theory of property. Clement, however, examines the parable of the rich young ruler to whom the Lord said, ' Sell that thou hast and give to the poor '; and by an interpretation that may stray far from the original sense but is good evidence of his own thought, argues that wealth itself is external and morally indifferent. Only internal states harm a man. In truth Christ wanted the youth to rid himself of wrong passions. He demands the right use of wealth, not renunciation as such. Property frees us from worry about external things, so that we can devote ourselves to things of the spirit, and enables us to help others. If no one has possessions, how can there be any fellowship (*koinonia*, sharing) between men? Here is the germ of a theory recognizing intrinsic value in private property, and some understanding that anxiety over elementary necessities may frustrate the development of higher values.

Again, early Christians commonly esteemed celibacy above marriage. Clement opposes this tendency, finding positive values in the married state, insisting on the spiritual training which comes to a husband and a father and suggesting that a father 'actually preserves a faint image of the true Providence'.

Nevertheless, Clement was not, in any modern sense, a liberal humanist. When he finds value in property and marriage, it is not because he reckons the things which money will buy good in themselves or because human love is to him an absolute good. He values them for their moral discipline. At bottom, he has his own type of other-worldliness. Most men, he believed, must be content to live by faith and works. God intends them to live a practical life in the world. With regard to these men Clement is comparatively liberal and humanist. But there are others, 'more elect than the elect', to whom God vouchsafes the true Christian life of contemplation. For them the moral ideal is 'apathy', freedom from worldly desires. And Clement had no doubt that this life is intrinsically higher than the most praiseworthy practical behaviour, so that, at what he must have considered the deepest level of his thought, he advocated withdrawal from the world.

The moral rigorism of Tertullian, tempered by Cyprian and other practical minds, appealed greatly to the stronger Christian spirits, ready if need be to undergo martyrdom. Clement's intellectualism and contemplative ideal, which were also to become permanent elements in the Christian outlook, were open to but few. The ordinary Christian was taught by his clergy to pursue in his daily life the straightforward biblical virtues, to be honest, just and charitable, to cultivate a forgiving and peaceable temper. The bitterest critic of Christian practice will scarcely claim that such teaching is anti-social. In these early centuries the Church could not attack, much less alter, social institutions. It could not stop war, overthrow slavery or relieve economic distress by fundamental changes in economic structure. No doubt its chief sphere of influence was the family. But any reader of St. Paul's letter to Philemon will see how slavery could be transformed before its abolition. The runaway thief, now a Christian, is sent back to his Christian master 'no longer as a slave, but more than a slave, a brother beloved, specially to me, but how much rather to thee, both in the flesh and in the Lord'. Cicero had asked no more than that the slave should be treated as decently as the free employee. The truth is that the civilizing power of Christianity had first to be demonstrated on a small scale in and through those who were genuinely possessed of the Christian spirit.

Similarly, Christian charity had to be built up internally before Christian institutions could furnish a stimulus or pattern to the State. Tertullian tells how Christians who suffered for their faith became the 'pensioners of their confession', how Christian alms went to feed and bury the poor and to care for orphans, old slaves and shipwrecked sailors. The pagan Lucian, poking fun at the simple-minded Christians, laughs at the benevolence which could so easily be cheated. In the *Didascalia*, which describes the organization of the Church in Syria during the third century, we find instructions for the supervision of orphans. The bishop is to get them adopted, to arrange marriages for the girls and to provide for the training of the boys in a craft, encouraging self-help. When plague broke out over Africa just after the harsh persecution instituted by Decius (250-251), there was a general flight, but Christians stayed to tend the sick and bury the dead. The same thing happened in Egypt soon after the next great persecution under Valerian. In each case the evidence (admittedly Christian) is that the pagans abandoned any attempt at 'social service'.

No doubt these acts of charity were palliatives and no substitute for organized social action through the State. Nor was charity a Christian monopoly. But State action has usually followed individual experiment, and it cannot be an accident or coincidence that State social services have been most far-reaching in countries which have the Christian tradition behind them, even if they have now rejected it. Many such services are simply the nationalization of Christian works of charity.

The Christian Empire

In A.D. 313, by what is usually called the Edict of Milan, the emperors Constantine and Licinius brought persecution to an end. Formally, the Christian faith was given legal recognition on a par with other cults; in fact, Constantine became a Christian, favoured the Church and took the first steps towards the suppression of pagan cults and the establishment of Christianity, a policy brought to fulfilment under Theodosius at the end of the century. The Church was faced with new opportunities and new dangers. Its morale, kept at a high level by the sternly selective process of persecution (though the early Church must not be idealized), might drop as the faith became fashionable. Other-worldliness might not survive fuller contact with this world, with fuller social responsibility, not to mention ease and wealth. On the other hand here was the chance to preach and teach on an altogether new scale, to baptize the whole life of the empire whether by the indirect influence of individual Christians or directly by pressure upon the central organs of the State.

If perfect laws alone will not create a perfect society, good legislation is an outward sign of social improvement and an aid towards establishing the external conditions of moral progress. Constantine's legislation was manifold and largely beneficent. Attacking the old Roman custom of exposing unwanted infants to the benevolence or malevolence of a passer-by, he made provision for the children of the poor by sanctioning official gifts of food, clothing and money to needy parents and by encouraging adoption. He enhanced the legal protection of minors. Manumission of slaves became easier, especially to the Church, and the breaking up of their families on the sale of estates was forbidden. Prison conditions were improved and several barbarous punishments reduced or forbidden. It cannot, of course, be argued that all valuable social legislation in the later Roman empire was Christian in inspiration. In Constantine's case, however, the evidence is substantial and, besides the fact that bishops such as Eusebius of Caesarea and Hosius of Cordova are known to have been among his intimate advisers, can be seen in the laws themselves. For example, branding upon the face is forbidden to prevent the mutilation of 'the face which is fashioned after the likeness of the heavenly beauty'—a manifestly Christian touch. The exclusion of divorce for light reasons and the new and heavy penalties inflicted for sexual offences are certainly due to Christian influence. Their value, indeed their propriety, may be questioned, but they are excellent evidence that the State was influenced by the Christian point of view. And both Church and State deserve credit for their attempt to raise the standard of sexual morality in the empire.

Apart from legislation or social work under government control, Christian charity now swelled into a mighty stream. Even in A.D. 303 the Church of Cirta (now Constantine), a modest city in North Africa, possessed a considerable stock of clothing for charitable distribution—eighty-two women's garments, sixteen for men, thirty-eight *mafortea* (veils?), thirteen pairs of men's shoes, forty-seven of women's, eighteen clogs for the country. As its wealth grew, it was taken for granted that the Church would care for the poor. As early as A.D. 251, the Church of Rome had fifteen hundred widows and distressed persons on its maintenance roll. Antioch supported three thousand and Constantinople seven thousand at the close of the following century. Monasteries, at first dependent upon charity, became its dispensers, as we know from the hospital and other works attached to St. Basil's monastery at Caesarea in Cappadocia, the prototype of most Greek monasticism. To multiply examples would be unsatisfactory since their representative character may be challenged. Perhaps the best proof of the impact made by Christian benevolence upon society in the fourth century lies in the instructions which the apostate emperor Julian gave to his provincial governors and to the pagan priests whom he expected to lead the revival of Hellenic paganism. 'That Hellenism does not succeed as we wish,' he wrote to the High Priest of Galatia, 'is owing to those who profess it. . . . It is not enough for you only to be blameless. Intreat or compel all the priests in Galatia to be virtuous. . . . Admonish every priest not to frequent the theatre or drink in taverns or exercise any mean and disgraceful trade or employment. Honour those who obey you; expel those who disobey you. Erect also hospitals in every city. . . . For when none of the Jews beg and the impious Galileans (i.e. Christians) relieve both their own poor and ours, it is shameful that ours should be destitute of our assistance.' And elsewhere, describing the kind of priest he desires, 'A proof of his love for his fellows is his sharing cheerfully, even from a small store, with those in need and giving willingly thereof and trying to do good to as many men as he is able. We must pay special attention to this point and by this means effect a cure. For when it came about that the poor were neglected and overlooked by the priests, then I think the impious Galileans observed this fact and devoted themselves to philanthropy, and they have gained ascendancy in the worst of their deeds through the credit they win for such practices.' A Christian comment on Julian's policy comes from the distinguished theologian Gregory of Nazianzus, who had attended the University of Athens with him. 'Julian was intending to build inns and hospices for pilgrims, monasteries for men, convents for virgins, places for meditation, and to establish a system of charity for the relief of prisoners, and also the method of letters of commendation by which we forward such as require it from one nation to another—all things which he had especially admired in our institutions.'[2] The same imitation of Christian philanthropy has been observed in lands where missionaries are at work; and indeed the development of social services by secular States illustrates the same principle, though hostility to religion may be absent.

Sheer lack of evidence makes it impossible to measure with any precision how far society was improved by the activity of Christian laymen in public life. Moreover, the empire was already declining to its fall, the economic life of the fourth century was chaotic, there was much border warfare and not a little internal rebellion. Christians were still a minority in most places and those in high positions were not always the most sincere. What is abundantly clear is the social importance of the bishop; and the evidence of his activity often illustrates simultaneously the value of a Christian magistrate.

Ever since St. Paul's admonition to the Corinthians, Christians had endeavoured to settle disputes amicably without resort to litigation. In time the bishop's 'court' became the instrument of such arbitration, at first purely among the faithful. Then Constantine took a step of great consequence when he decided to bring the episcopal courts within the judicial system of the State. Civil cases, he enacted, might be transferred from secular to episcopal courts, and the bishop's decision should be final. The extent of episcopal jurisdiction varied from time to time, and the details are sometimes obscure. There is no doubt that their courts were popular. Their speed and fairness were contrasted with the corruption and sloth of the ordinary courts—and they were free! St. Augustine spent many weary hours over his judicial work, hours which he coveted for spiritual exercises and theological study. But he recognized the importance of this duty. A parallel function of bishops was the right of intercession, that is, of taking up cases with magistrates to secure justice or to plead for mercy. This right was frequently exercised (for instance by St. Augustine), especially in order to mitigate a death sentence.

The extant letters of several bishops admirably illustrate their secular opportunities. St. Basil, Bishop of Caesarea (370-379), and St. Augustine, Bishop of Hippo (395-430), may be taken as examples. As metropolitan of Cappadocia, Basil was in constant touch with imperial officials, to whom some sixty of his surviving letters are addressed. Some were written to tax-collectors, asking for consideration for the heavily burdened or exhorting to just dealing. Once he writes to the Prefect's Accountant, asking him to discuss plans for poor relief, to inspect the hospital for the poor in his district and to exempt it from taxation. One Christian magistrate is highly praised—'the most incorruptible man I know, a true guardian of justice'. Sophronius, Master of the Offices and later Prefect of Constantinople, received many requests from him, as did Modestus, Prefect of the East. Count Helladius is asked to assist a widow, hard pressed by the guardians of her husband's heirs. It is quite clear that the bishop could, and did, exercise much influence for good; and it is equally clear that many magistrates were by this time Christian, were prepared to listen sympathetically to the intercession of the Church, and were personally men whom Basil highly respected.

St. Augustine, too, though no metropolitan, had much business with officials. At one moment he writes scathingly to denounce the pagan magistrates of Sufes for allowing the murder of sixty Christians, at another he pleads with a Christian judge not to carry out a sentence of death upon the Donatist murderers of a Catholic priest. On one occasion a pagan magistrate of Calama, whose citizens had illegally celebrated pagan festivals, thereby causing a riot, asked the bishop to shield the offenders from the due rigours of the law. Another group of letters illustrates the law of sanctuary and the bishop's vigorous response to a breach of it. A military official had, quite illegally, abducted a certain Faventius who had taken refuge in the church at Hippo. Immediately Augustine gets another officer to search for him, and follows this action up with letters to a neighbouring bishop and a magistrate in which the story is narrated, making clear the exact breaches of the law. These are no isolated examples. To champion the poor and oppressed was so much part of a bishop's life that the State itself looked to him for help in maintaining or tempering justice as occasion demanded. We may take leave of Augustine as he counsels Count Boniface, commander of Roman forces in Africa, not to abandon his duty in the world for 'spiritual' reasons. 'Do not think it impossible for a soldier to please God.' It is right for him to defend Africa against barbarian violence. 'We must not *before the time* desire to live with the saints alone.'[3]

The Social Theory

Many Christians, however, did desire to live with the saints alone. As Christianity became the normal religion, it was hard to keep up the old intensity; as numbers grew it was hard even to teach the elements of faith and discipline, harder still to preserve an other-worldly spirit when the business of the world had increasingly to be carried on by Christians and when the clergy were grappling with a host of new social responsibilities. Serious Christians were disturbed and re-action showed itself in two principal ways. First, there was schism, the cry for a pure church, an exclusive church of saints. This was one aspect of Donatism, a powerful move-ment in Latin Africa which continued the Puritan strain in the Montanist and Novatianist schisms and stood for the rigorous application of Christian discipline and the expulsion of gross sinners from the Church, in opposition to the tendency towards charity (laxity, they called it) and the concept of the Church as a school for sinners. The second way was asceti-cism, whether domestic, as among the patrician ladies of Rome who are portrayed in Jerome's letters, or monastic.

This is not the place for a history or an estimate of early monasticism. Enough for the moment to point out that while, on the one hand, it probably withdrew from 'social work', for example as Christian magistrates, many men of the highest character, on the other it provided a standing challenge to a worldly Church. If at first it cannot be acquitted of all escapism, it was to become a reservoir of spiritual energy for sincere Christians in the world as well as a civilizing agency of inestimable importance.

The Constantinian revolution had caught the Church with-out a considered theory of society. And so, while hermits fled from all such worldliness and the rank and file of the clergy pursued their daily tasks, the greater minds, an Ambrose, an Augustine, set themselves to meet the need. They were not working in a vacuum, nor could they wipe the slate clean to plan a wholly new world. Christianity came to power in a society (a rather aged and weary society) with settled forms and institutions. Since these had taken shape in a pagan world and were protected by a mature body of law, not itself erected upon Christian principles, and since it was plainly impossible to discard them totally without producing chaos, Christian thinkers were compelled to ask themselves how much of them they could accept in principle and in practice, and in what new directions they must point. After all, there was much to be said for some Roman institutions. Rome had great political experience. Stoicism, though it had failed to invigorate the common man, had taught much that is true and noble, and above all there was Roman law and jurisprudence. Christian social thought treated this inheritance with respect. It is significant that one of its chief expositions, the *De Officiis* [On Duties] of St. Ambrose, is modelled on Cicero's work of the same title; and a great deal of accepted principle could be taken over by Christians under the notion of natural law. So with regard to the main practices of government, the teachings of Roman law, the institutions of war, slavery and private property, the Church of the late Roman Empire was predominantly conservative, often too conservative. Yet, at bottom, there was at least one vital difference. Whereas pagan Rome believed these institutions to be fully natural, to Christians they were the result of the Fall. Thus, while society itself is natural since men are created for fellowship with each other, coercive government is God's remedy for the unruliness of fallen human nature. So with slavery. 'By nature, as God first created us, no one is the slave either of man or of sin,' said St. Augustine. 'The prime cause of slavery is sin which lays man under the dominion of his fellow.' Chrysostom, who may be allowed to represent the opinion of the Eastern Church, is in full agreement. War also is the result of sin, and, according to Ambrose, private property would be unnecessary in a truly natural (i.e. unfallen) society.

Explanation of social institutions in terms of the Fall had a double and paradoxical effect. Since grace transforms fallen nature, there must always be the possibility of 'progress', so that Utopian hopes revive continually in Christian history. Running contrary to this, however, was the even stronger conviction that true happiness will never be complete in this world, that these social institutions, though the result of sin, have been brought within the divine plan either as punishments or as ordinances necessary to control sin, in either case to be accepted as the appointed environment or raw material of moral development. Hence the spirit of Christian resignation, the despair of social reformers, a spirit so easily perverted into complacency or hypocrisy, precious as it is in its highest form. For no enthusiasm for amenities, no recognition that the soul is not to be divorced from the body, should deceive us into thinking that spiritual health is mathematically proportionate to material well-being.

Accepting such theories, the Church was largely thrown back upon philanthropy, with a success in that limited sphere which its best-informed critics have generously recognized. Slavery remained, but thousands of slaves were manumitted and thousands more were better treated. The status of women improved, hospitals (a Christian development from rudimentary anticipations) sprang up, the care of foundlings was transferred to the Church, every diocese had its roll of the poor and needy. That the Church had little or no applicable economic theory is only too true; but no one else had. Again, if pacifism was repudiated, the grounds of a just war were explored and delimited. The Christian denunciation of all aggressive war was a clear advance upon the international ethics of the ancient world.

It is hard to pass judgement upon Christian social effort in the later Roman Empire since one has to consider not only what success it had in those things which it sought to do (and here the evidence is incomplete), but also how far its omissions were culpable and what difficulties or opposition it had to surmount. Its endeavours were not limited only by the Fall-theory of social institutions. Behind that lay a deep-seated other-worldliness which shrank from secular concerns, and the easily distorted ' spirituality ' which counted bodily needs and pleasures of no worth, if not temptations to evil. But even if all Christians had striven for social progress, they would still have been a minority, supported, it is true, by most emperors, but far from controlling every organ of administration or every means of influencing public opinion. The Roman senate, for instance, was largely, and even aggressively, pagan at the end of the fourth century. Within, the Church was hampered by insincere converts, including worldly bishops, and was compelled to devote much of its energy and thought to doctrinal controversy. In short, there was so much else to do. Above all, there was the obstacle of ordinary human sin. It is quite ridiculous to evaluate Christian social ' success ' in terms of an unrealistic estimate of human nature which Christian faith itself repudiates. The ecclesiastical authorities of the period under consideration knew the material with which they must work and understood that they could only proceed piecemeal. It was not their proper function, and never is the proper function of ecclesiastical authority as such, to produce a blue-print of the perfect society and to demand that secular authority should enforce it. Limited by the circumstances of their day, they achieved much which paganism had not even attempted. Possibly a more striking immediate result could have been attained if they had concentrated all their energies upon semi-political activities at the expense of their evangelistic and pastoral obligations. Had they done so, not only the Church but the world would have suffered in the long run.

There was another paradoxical consequence of the early Christian attitude to the State. Since State action had never been considered a manifestation of love, many Christians actually preferred charity (which is love) to State services. A generation which is seeing the depersonalizing effects of highly elaborate State services may discover that individual and voluntary service is not to be scorned as a mere palliative. On the other hand, reflection upon the ever thorny issue of the relations between Church and State, such as we find at its most profound in St. Augustine, who based it upon the more ultimate distinction between the Two Cities of God and of this world, produced an attempt to distinguish the spheres of Church and State and, on the assumption that the sovereign would henceforth be a Christian, bound by a Christian concept of justice, to leave secular concerns to secular authority. True, the ruler was in principle open to ecclesiastical criticism on moral grounds, but in practice the Church must often have taken the easy line of minding its own business.

Imperial favour brought with it a considerable danger that the Church would become unduly subject to the State. Doubtless there were courtier bishops; the Eastern Church has often been blamed for its subservience. Yet in both East and West examples of independence abound. How Ambrose humbled the powerful Emperor Theodosius when he had ordered the massacre at Thessalonica has been told so often as perhaps to create an impression that Christians have no other instance to quote. But Basil of Caesarea defied Valens, Martin of Tours challenged Maximus, Chrysostom vituperated the court of Constantinople, and Hosius of Cordova, once Constantine's confidential adviser, wrote thus to his successor Constantius: ' Intrude not yourself into ecclesiastical matters, neither give commands unto us concerning them, but learn them from us. God hath put into your hands the kingdom: to us He hath entrusted the affairs of His Church; and, as he who should steal the empire from you would resist the ordinance of God, so likewise fear on your part lest, by taking upon yourself the government of the Church, you become guilty of a great offence.'[4] And not Athanasius alone, but a great company of bishops preferred exile to imperial perversions of the faith.

If those to whom the sole criterion of a religion's value is social progress suspect social complacency or irresponsibility in the Christian's concern with theological truth, with faith, worship and the world to come, they must try to understand that it was precisely this ultimate other-worldliness which enabled Ambrose and his like to stand unshaken against the secular omnipotence of a Roman emperor.

II

The Barbarian Invasions and the Early Middle Ages

IF the Roman Empire had survived, would Christianity have transformed its social life with the inevitability of gradualness? No man can answer the great ifs of history. In this case, Byzantium cannot tell us, for its own development was necessarily modified by the break-up of the West. After a fierce struggle with its own barbarian invaders and after the partial and transitory success of Justinian's reconquest of the West, the Eastern Empire was left alone to face Islam. It dwindled, but held fast, a bulwark of Christianity and culture until the close of the Middle Ages.

While almost any German historian will proclaim the virtues of the Teutonic invaders, almost any French scholar will deplore the overthrow of Latin culture, plunged into the darkness of night by northern barbarism. To see a truth between these extremes (verging perhaps towards the French view) is not merely an English will to compromise. It may be that Europe needed a breath of something robust and vigorous, some new conception of freedom. But vigour manifested itself too often as brutality, robustness as scorn for the refinements of culture, and freedom as licence for the powerful without protection for the weak. Sometimes, too, the invaders were quicker to pick up the vices of 'civilization' than its virtues.

In A.D. 378 the Goths defeated the Emperor Valens at Hadrianople. Failing to take the walled city of Constantinople, they turned north-west, conquered parts of the Balkan peninsula and moved farther west, only to be barred from Italy in 405 by the imperial general Stilicho. In 406 the Vandals, Suevi and Alans crossed the Rhine into Gaul and hurried on into Spain. Roman troops were withdrawn from Britain, which fell to the Angles and Saxons a generation later. In 410 Alaric's Visigoths sacked Rome and occupied southern Italy, but withdrew to set up kingdoms in Gaul and Spain. In 429 the Vandals conquered Latin Africa. Though Attila and his Huns were turned back in 451, Burgundians, Alemans and Franks took their share of Gaul. The last emperor of the West was deposed in 476; in 493 Italy became an Ostrogothic kingdom under Theodoric.

What was to be the religion and therefore the civilization of these new kingdoms? The answer lay with the Christian Church alone. Some of the invaders came with a veneer of Christianity (a veneer not because they had been converted by Arians, but because their new faith had not gone deep), others were wholly pagan. It was a major turning-point in history when the pagan Clovis accepted orthodox Christianity for himself and his Franks. By this move he won the support of Rome and of the remaining Gallo-Roman population against the Arian kingdoms in Gaul, and so was enabled to conquer the whole country. The conversion of the Franks, nominal at first, gave the Church her opportunity. Anyone who contrasts Gregory of Tours' description of Merovingian Gaul with Charlemagne's empire (with all its faults) will apprehend something of the civilizing power of the Christian faith. Here, if anywhere, is progress which cannot be attributed to technological advance.

There was, of course, a preliminary issue, and no small one. Though rooted in Semitic religion, Christianity had won its chief victories as it moved west. Its theology had absorbed much Greek philosophy and its organization largely coincided with that of the Roman Empire. It might seem a mere aspect of Graeco-Roman culture. Was it now to die with this culture? Or would that culture prove to be the temporary vesture of an eternal and potentially universal religion? As to-day India, China or Africa receives the same religion from western missionaries, we ask whether its Christianity will shake off any inessential trappings and take new national forms without losing its essence. In principle, the answer has been given already, for Christianity converted the barbarians and transformed their lives not as a mere vehicle of the ancient culture, but as the informing spirit of a new civilization.

The Bishops and the Barbarians

The means by which the transformation was accomplished were both outward or institutional and inward or spiritual. Outwardly the principal agents were the episcopate, culminating in the papacy, and the monks. Inwardly we may distinguish the preservation of learning, the fight for morality, missionary preaching, and spirituality in its technical sense— worship, prayer and the culture of the soul.

The contribution made by the bishops to the civilization of the early Middle Ages can hardly be exaggerated. 'The life of the capital of the civitas,' wrote Ferdinand Lot, 'depended from Merovingian times on the bishop; its material as well as its spiritual existence was concentrated in his hands. Moreover, this was a general phenomenon. The preponderance of the episcopate is found everywhere, in Italy, in Egypt and in the East.' Again, 'the Church was one of the organs of the State, indeed the only fairly reliable one.'[1] Some functions fell to the bishops in virtue of the lands belonging to their sees, others were the responsibilities (at least to a Christian mind) of wealth. Thus the bishop was by law responsible for the maintenance of his city's aqueducts and fortifications, and was expected to store grain against times of famine. 'Felix of Nantes constructed embankments against the flooding of the Loire; a bishop of Mainz dammed the Rhine; Didier of Cahors restored the fortifications of the town.'[2] Sidonius Apollinaris, Bishop of Clermont, whose letters tell us so much of life in Gaul at the end of the fifth century, writes to Bishop Patiens of Lyons in 474, 'When the Gothic ravages were over and the crops were all destroyed by fire, you distributed corn to the destitute throughout all the ruined land of Gaul at your own expense. . . . I cannot exactly tell the sum of gratitude which all the people owe you, inhabitants of Arles and Riez,

C

Avignon, Orange, Viviers, Valence and Trois Chateaux. . . .
But for the city of Clermont I can speak.'[3]

Still other duties arose from the State's readiness to take the
bishops into partnership. The judicial functions inaugurated
by Constantine were much increased. In Gaul, from 614, the
bishop alone had authority in civil cases proper, such as
admitted of a monetary composition. Besides, they were able
to co-operate with, or if necessary withstand, the Counts, who
were the chief judicial officers of the Frankish kingdom.
O. M. Dalton, a high authority on this period, writes, 'Had
the activities of the Church been suddenly extinguished in the
Gaul of the sixth century, the lawlessness which already threatened the foundations of social life would have been freed from
the sole permanent restraining force; the country would have
sunk into irremediable anarchy.'[4]

Gaul has been quoted since the existing evidence allows a
more complete picture here than elsewhere of the Church's
struggle with the barbarians. But the bishop's influence was
everywhere considerable. In England he sat with the ealdor-
man in the shire courts, while the bishops collectively took
their place in the King's Council, the Witan. That the unity
of the English kingdom was promoted by the earlier unity of
the English Church, especially by the work of Theodore
of Tarsus, Archbishop of Canterbury (668-690), has been
generally acknowledged. And it was not necessary to be a
Theodore. Professor Stenton tells of the work of one whose
name few will know, Waldhere, Bishop of London, in 704 or
705. Addressing to Archbishop Berhtwald 'the first letter
known to have been written by one Englishman to another',
he 'states that he has been invited to a council shortly to be
held at Brentford for the settlement of disputes between the
kings of Essex and the king of Wessex, in which ecclesiastical
persons are involved. His presence is needed because the
kings have promised to observe whatever form of agreement
he and the West Saxon bishop may devise. . . . He adds that
he has recently refused the invitation of Cenred, king of
Mercia, to a council summoned to deal with the "reconcilia-

tion " of a certain Aelfthryth, because he did not know the archbishop's mind in the matter. This document . . . shows the
influence which a bishop might exert as a mediator at such a
time, and the respect of the lay world for the bishop's office.'[5]
Meanwhile in the Christian East, to give but one instance, the
whole care of prisons was entrusted to the bishops by the laws
of Justinian.

It is not claimed that everything which the bishops did was
good, but that we cannot dissociate such progress as was made
from official Christian advice, sought and given as part of a
bishop's duty. That there were no bad bishops would be
beyond belief, even if we had no evidence of them. The power
which they exercised and the wealth which they possessed were
standing temptations. Moreover, their influence in secular
affairs made it imperative for kings to control their appointment and often, no doubt, to choose the wrong man.

But the independence displayed by Ambrose was not a thing
of the past. To quote Dalton again : ' A bishop of unsullied
repute could carry matters with a high hand even against the
king, as when Nicetius of Trèves refused to say mass before
King Theuderic because of his offences; or when Germanus
of Paris excommunicated King Charibert for marrying a
nun. . . . Episcopal majesty was further enhanced by the fact
that when it came to a real trial of strength, a resolute bishop
could more often intimidate a king than a king a bishop; the
kings, who stood in awe of no laymen, were generally afraid
of churchmen, treating them as a rule with a respect shown to
no other class, not even the most powerful members of the
Teutonic aristocracy.'[6]

The Influence of Monasticism

While the bishop engaged in the rough and tumble of
political and social life and no doubt was coarsened by its
roughness, the monastery stood behind him as a source of
light. It cannot be allowed that monasteries should be judged
primarily by their social consequences, certainly not by their
material and cultural gifts to the world. They were not

founded for such purposes; and if we are to look at all beyond
their proper work, the *opus Dei*, worship, to any effect upon
other men, the Christian will think first of their intercessory
prayer and of their contribution to the inner life of the Church
through the practice and study of worship and spirituality.
Nevertheless, monasticism has brought rich gifts of other kinds
to society, especially during these centuries of darkness and
strife. In them, more than anywhere else, ancient learning was
preserved and many useful crafts were learned and taught;
agriculture in particular benefited.

Early western monasticism tended to follow the Egyptian
model, more ascetic and more individualistic than the Basilian
type which had become popular in much of the East. However, as the Rule of St. Benedict (A.D. 526) came to prevail,
western monasteries changed in character. As Dom Butler
says of Benedict, 'Nothing probably was further from his
thoughts than that his monks were to become apostles,
bishops, popes, civilizers, educators, scholars, men of learning.
His idea simply was to make them good; and if a man is good,
he will do good.'[7]   And so it came to pass, partly because of
Benedict's insistence on a large measure of work, besides worship, in the daily life of the monk. Some became scholars,
some administrators, some gave themselves to works of charity,
others—in early days the majority—got on with the hard work
of the fields from which the monastery won its daily bread.
In this way a chain of inns, hospitals, foundling homes, old
people's homes and other institutions[8] sprang up over Europe
on a scale which, outstripping the category of private charity,
approximates to a modern 'social service'. Further, as forests
were cleared (e.g. by the monasteries of Jumièges and Fon-
tenelle), land was cultivated and vineyards planted, so that
the monks were very frequently the instructors of the peasant,
as well as examples of the dignity of labour, no longer to be
despised as servile. The greater houses played an important
part (though at some cost to their religious life) in the development of communications and commerce, while many a town
grew up under the shelter of a monastery (e.g. Abingdon, St.

Albans, Bury St. Edmunds). 'As early as the eighth century agents for the French monasteries were active in Flanders purchasing wool for manufacture. In the wine trade of Burgundy it was the monasteries that were the important centres; and abbeys on the Loire and Seine owned a fleet of river vessels for conducting their trade. In Florence the wool industry is said to have dated from the settlement of a monastic order, the Umiliati, in 1238; the work being done by lay brothers under the superintendence of priests. In England the earliest establishment of German traders seems to have been an order of monks.'[9]

That the monks had their faults is beyond dispute. Their very occupation with secular business, still more their success in it, was morally dangerous. But their contribution to the civilization of Europe cannot be questioned by any who accept the necessity and the over-all benefit of the growth of commerce.

All such outward-facing activity, episcopal or monastic, was an outgrowth from the inner life. It is not pertinent to this book to describe the worship of the Church or the spiritual nurture of the individual. Enough to insist that without them the other could not have been done. Nor will it be possible to give more than the barest indication of the geographical expansion which went on in Europe while elsewhere Christianity was losing ground to Islam. One by one the Teutonic tribes were converted from their Arianism or paganism—Burgundians, Franks, Goths, Lombards. British Christianity, kept alive in Ireland, joined hands with Rome to evangelize the Anglo-Saxons; later Irish and Anglo-Saxon monks became the apostles of Germany and the North. The missionary work of Boniface in the eighth century and his reform of the Frankish Church was an indispensable preliminary to the Carolingian renaissance. In the ninth century Moravia, Bulgaria and other Slavonic regions accepted the Christian faith. Most of this work was disinterested missionary enterprise, undertaken by heroic spirits at the risk of their lives; and although Charlemagne's forcible conversion of the Saxons under pain of death was wicked, their true Christianization had still to be effected by peaceful means.

Education and Morality

Two elements in the work of civilization (which it seems absurd to think of as ecclesiastical 'interference') need special attention, namely learning and moral training. The Church should not aspire to unqualified praise for its preservation of ancient learning. So much was not preserved. Still, when all qualifications are made, the contrast with barbarism is plain enough. If the Church cared for some branches of learning only, and for its own purposes, few of the invaders cared for it at all. Witness the difference between Ireland, which escaped the invasions to become the cradle of restored European learning, and England which, wholly paganized, had to recover learning from Ireland and Rome. Even Northern Italy, conquered by the Lombards, had to be revived by scholars from Ireland and a renewed England.

To the early Church the use of pagan learning and literature was long a hard case of conscience. First, Greek philosophy was suspect. St. Paul warns his converts against the wisdom of this world. What has Jerusalem to do with Athens? cried Tertullian. Was this obscurantism? Perhaps, if Christianity had *persisted* in refusing to take any account of secular thought. But it was necessary first that Christians should clearly understand that their faith was not just one more philosophy, to be judged solely by the standards of philosophy, but a revelation, a *divinum negotium* as Tertullian called it, that is, something that God has done, something with its own specific sources and authorities. In the event, Origen, followed by Jerome and Augustine, decided to 'spoil the Egyptians', using Greek thought in the service of Christian theology. This policy commended itself to majority opinion in the Church, so that much pagan learning was preserved, even if the books lay long unread in some cathedral or monastic library. In any case, pagan philosophy was not proscribed and pagan philosophers were not persecuted by the

early Church. Long before Justinian closed the Schools of
Athens in 529 they had shot their bolt. After Plotinus
the great thinkers were Christian, and that not accident-
ally but essentially. Philosophy was renewed by faith and
paganism out-thought. 'Unless ye believe, ye shall not
understand.'

The imaginative literature of Greece and Rome was both
loved and feared, loved because Christians, like other men,
had a sense of beauty, and feared partly because the Church
was slow to come to terms with beauty, but mainly because it
was pagan. A world which is impregnated with Christian
thought can stand a good deal of pagan literature; a Church
which is struggling out of a pagan environment may well decide to make a clean cut. The rationalist of to-day has his
own gods, to whom he is often in greater bondage than he
realizes, but at least he does not believe in the gods of Homer
and Virgil. Many early Christians had only just ceased to
worship them, and second thoughts were dangerously possible.
Fortunately, however, the risk was taken by men who saw
that exponents of Christianity had much to learn from the
literary and rhetorical powers of the ancients. So Cicero and
Quintilian were in favour in the West, together with nearly
all the Latin poets, not excluding Ovid. The grammarians
were naturally valued, as well as the practical writers, medical,
veterinary or agricultural. In pure science there was scarcely
any interest, a fault not specific to Christians at that time.
The study of Roman Law, as codified by Theodosius and
Justinian, continued in Italy, but the books of the older
lawyers, apparently superfluous, survived (if at all) by very
tenuous threads.

It must be confessed, then, that the early Christian attitude
to learning was lukewarm and utilitarian. That does not alter
the fact that we owe what did survive in the West to the
Church and especially to the monasteries; and it is to be
supposed that many a scholar, sheltered under the official
approval of useful letters, was inwardly devoted to learning
for its own sake. By the time of Charlemagne a first

renaissance of culture, with its roots in Irish and English ecclesiastical scholarship, had come into being.

Education, as well as learning, was almost a monopoly of the Church. Under the Empire, when Christians could receive a secular education in the schools of the State, the Church itself had concentrated upon the training of the clergy. St. Augustine's *De Doctrina Christiana* shows that hard thinking was devoted to this subject. In Italy public schools and lay scholarship survived the invasions, providing teachers for other lands, if few scholars of note. But perhaps it would be no great exaggeration to say that the renewal of lay education elsewhere was a by-product of the demand for a literate clergy. Early in the period we meet the great name of Cassiodorus, adviser to Theodoric, the Ostrogothic King of Italy. When political disturbances had frustrated his dream of a Christian university at Rome, Cassiodorus, retired in old age from public life, founded a monastery at Vivarium (*c*. A.D. 540). Here he not only collected the famous library which was destined to be one of the principal means of the survival of the classics, but also worked out in his *Institutes* an educational system which, though intended to produce theologians, was based upon the seven liberal arts—grammar, rhetoric and dialectic, arithmetic, music, astronomy and geometry. By this means he introduced into Benedictinism a learned note which has never left it and, at the same time, determined the educational method of the Middle Ages.

For the next two centuries learning was rare in continental Europe, though very much alive in the British Isles. Episcopal schools existed for boys who were intended for the priesthood from an early age. Monastic schools similarly catered for their own oblates, and to some small extent for children of the nobility. But if a Christian civilization was to be established, as Charlemagne intended, education must be more widely spread. Clerical literacy in particular was essential not only for the spiritual welfare and moral training of the people, but also for the fulfilment of the numerous administrative duties which, alike at the centre of government and locally, were entrusted to bishop and priest. Charlemagne's policy can be studied in his capitularies in which the priest is told to instruct his people and the abbot his monks. Bishops were exhorted or ordered to improve the episcopal schools and 'higher' education was provided for in the Palace school at Aachen, directed by the English scholar Alcuin. Elementary education depended on the enthusiasm of individual bishops, as when Leidrad of Lyons reports the opening of schools in his diocese or Theodulf of Orleans orders his priests in towns and villages to keep schools to which children may be sent without any compulsory fee.

The content and purpose of Carolingian education was Christian. At the higher level, the arts led to theology, though many clerics spent their time as civil administrators; at the lower stage, children would learn the elements of their religion. 'Let them be taught the Creed, the Lord's Prayer and the Ten Commandments,' Charlemagne said. Theodulf presumably intended something more by his 'let them learn letters'. Letters means Latin, the first step in an education reaching far beyond elementary and oral catechetical instruction in the vernacular.

Though Charlemagne's high aims met with serious setbacks after his death, especially in his own lands, they were renewed in England by King Alfred. An English culture should flower from the Latin root, English free-born boys should go to school until they could at least read English writing, while those who were to become priests should learn Latin. For the benefit of the parish priest Alfred translated the *Cura Pastoralis* [Pastoral Care] of Gregory the Great into English. This 'was for many centuries regarded as a manual for the guidance of the parish priest. But to Alfred its chief significance lay in its insistence on the bishops' responsibility for the instruction of the laity. The success of Alfred's own educational design depended on the assiduity of his bishops in teaching, and in seeking out the youths and children from whom the teachers of the next generation could be drawn.'[10]

The Christian monopoly of education has been turned

against the Church, which, it is sometimes said, has used it for its own ends at the expense of unfettered learning and free thought. Whether or not this is true of a later age, Charlemagne and Alfred knew what they were doing. The ordinary man of the early Middle Ages was not capable of free thought. He had to begin by learning that tradition of religion and morality through which civilization, barely enough, had survived. In all education, authority precedes freedom. At bottom, too, Charlemagne was aiming at the simplest moral necessities without which decent life, not to speak of learning, is impossible. And how great was that need is fully illustrated by the struggle of the Church with the northern invaders during the preceding centuries. Again we may turn for evidence to Charlemagne's own predecessors, the kings of Merovingian Gaul, whose characters are so vividly portrayed in the pages of Gregory of Tours. 'Clovis,' says Dalton, 'knew no pity; he destroyed any man who stood in the path of his ambition.' Theuderic, Chlodomer and Childebert were murderers. As to Chilperic, 'his lack of moral sense is so absolute that the occasional swerve towards decent conduct seems always the effect of chance, never of grace'. Even Guntram, who had good qualities, 'sullied his career by detestable acts of violence', executing his chamberlain for killing a wild ox in a royal forest. 'In private life he was somewhat less debauched than most Merovingian kings; cruel only in moments of sudden rage or panic.'

Among the queens, Fredegond 'moves before us like some primitive creature beyond the pale of the moral law, and full of cruel instincts'. 'Hers was a wickedness so elemental that we feel horror at the blank absence of honour, mercy, and the finer feelings.' The 'nobles' had every opportunity to follow these examples. 'The effect of freedom from all restraint is but too well exemplified by the actions of those among their number whose names are conspicuous in the *History*. The worst of all are Duke Rauching, who tortured his serfs while he sat at table, and even buried two of them alive because they decided to marry without his consent; the matricide

Eulalius; the drunken ravisher Amalo'—and so the tale goes on.[11] There have been bad kings and bad barons in plenty since those days, but such concentrated horror has rarely been known. Against that background, the bishops, despite the bad ones in their number, stand out as generally honourable, just and decent men who frequently defied those in high places, strove to defend their flocks against oppression and kept alive those elements of Christian morality without which there could be no higher civilization.

It is natural to ask whether the Church should have done even more during those dark centuries. So far as the Frankish realms are concerned, Dalton well brings out the dilemma of the bishops. 'To stand by the side of the Merovingian kings must have troubled the conscience of many a bishop; he fought in compromising company. To have the help of a Lothar was worse for the Church than to have the enmity of a Marcus Aurelius.'[12] Should they exchange co-operation with the State for sheer denunciation—and martyrdom? But when St. Columban, who came from outside, arraigned Queen Brunhild, 'the result was his expulsion from the kingdom and the loss of his leadership by those who could ill afford to be thus deprived'. They did what they could, in the actual circumstances. 'The abandonment by a conscientious bishop of his diocese would simply have led to the instalment of a more accommodating personality.' The moral is not so much that compromise is necessary, however dangerous, if the Church is to have any social responsibilities, as that no sensible judgement can be passed upon its success which takes no notice of the material with which it has to deal. To its labours, under God, and not to any inevitable progress, the Carolingian recovery was due; and if a happier example of co-operation between Church and State may readily be found in our own Alfred, none could be more dramatic and telling than the fortunes of Frankish Gaul.

III

The Later Middle Ages

THE flowering of the Carolingian Renaissance was but short. Dynastic quarrels, following upon the decision to carve up Charlemagne's empire among his sons, combined with the repeated and violent attacks of Saracens, Hungarians and Normans to bring in a century of regress, religious, moral, intellectual and economic, during which the counts took advantage of the decay of central authority to turn themselves into independent seigneurs or barons. The whole blame for this rapid disintegration must not be assigned to the attacks of external enemies, true though it is that the Frankish empire might have developed fast and well in a century of peace under a strong ruler. As it was, more than the brilliance of a single reign was required to impose a Christian culture upon peoples who were emerging from Merovingian darkness or who had been mass-converted (and sometimes by force) to a nominal Christianity. Charlemagne attempted to establish Christianity by legislation, partly by his own capitularies and partly by giving official sanction to the canon law of the Church. It was a noble vision in its way, but only the prolonged co-operation of parish priest and local magistrate could have taken it deep into the life of the people. How often has it happened that just when the Church has found its way to some ordered pattern of society, the conditions to which it was intended to apply have been radically transformed! So it was after Charlemagne.

In the centuries which followed him, the Church was still the principal instrument of recovery. 'In a society which had relapsed into general ignorance, it alone still retained those two indispensable instruments of culture, reading and writing, and it was from churchmen that kings and princes had necessarily to recruit their chancellors, their secretaries, their notaries, in short the whole lettered personnel, without which it was impossible for them to function. From the ninth century to the eleventh the whole business of government was, in fact, in the hands of the Church, which was supreme here, as in the arts. The organization of its estates was a model which the estates of the nobility sought in vain to equal, for only in the Church were there men capable of keeping registers of accounts, reckoning up receipts and expenditure, and, consequently, balancing them. Thus the Church was not only the great moral authority of the age, but also the great financial power. Moreover, the Church's conception of the world was admirably adapted to the economic conditions of an age in which land was the sole foundation of the social order.'[1]

From the nadir of the tenth century there is a crescendo of improvement up to the thirteenth, until over a large part of Europe something like a homogeneous Christendom had been established, in which the Church was so completely engaged in the life of society that it must take much of the credit and much of the blame for the ideals and practice of the age. It would show want of proportion to single out particular acts of intervention or interference; the Church was expected to formulate the moral basis of social institutions, in large measure to direct its application to daily life and constantly to call men to account for breaches of accepted laws. So brief a book as this can do little more than call attention to some of the principles by which the Church was guided, some of the dangers by which it was beset and some of the particular fields of action in which it sought to work. Of the latter, two will be discussed upon which the modern mind is wont to dwell, namely international affairs and economics.

First, however, we must understand how the Church had suffered from its struggle with the pre-Carolingian kingdoms. Fighting coarseness, it had itself been coarsened in ways which it was never able to throw off during its period of dominance. Compelled to treat most men, from king to serf, as turbulent or helpless children, it had developed an authoritarian habit which was not easily laid aside. Let us be more specific. To the Christian, politics and economics depend upon ethics, and ethics upon theology. Now, while the essence of the Christian faith can be apparent to the simple-hearted, its theology is not easy. Yet theology has to be taught, if only to the clergy. If we are not well acquainted with the theological attainments of the ordinary clergy of the fourth and fifth centuries, before the barbarian invasions, we do know with what profundity and intellectual subtlety the major issues of religious thought were debated by men such as Athanasius, the Cappadocian Fathers, Augustine and Cyril of Alexandria. Turn to Gregory the Great (Bishop of Rome, 590-604), whose works suffice to show what is meant by the coarsening of theology. They are rough and ready; delicacy is blunted, points have to be driven home with little care for refinement of thought. Already, too, there is a disquieting credulity, an eagerness to argue by appeal to the miraculous. That this should come about is easily understood, since the unruly Merovingian potentates, as we learn from Gregory of Tours, were cowed by nothing so much as the supernatural. With excellent intentions the Church grasped a weapon which would secure the allegiance of high and low alike. The obedient children should be told exactly how to live, their souls would be saved and society would prosper. Morality, therefore, was increasingly codified, both in the developing canon law and in the less formal penitentials which taught the clergy how to estimate—and punish—the relative gravity of sinful acts. All societies at some stages and some individuals throughout their lives have to be treated in this manner if there is to be an ordered community at all. Unfortunately the clergy have too often failed to recognize when the layman has grown up. Hence much anti-clericalism and secularism.

A totally different limitation of freedom hampered the Church itself. The very power which the State recognized in or conceded to the Church determined the State to control the Church. Charlemagne, who wanted a Christian empire, meant to rule it. Then, with the growth of the temporal wealth of the Church, especially in days when landlords were so much more than property-owners, it was imperative for a sovereign to demand some say in the choice of bishops. Consequently, throughout the centuries in which its influence was greatest, the Church, if not subjugated by the State, was for ever quarrelling with the secular rulers. There was a complete mutual involvement, but rarely a happy partnership.

The Clergy in Politics and Administration

The cardinal principle of medieval civilization, at least in theory, was the supremacy of the spiritual over the temporal and material; and the spiritual meant, in Europe, the Christian faith as taught by the Church. But how could this supremacy be assured in practice and by what organs? Though some thinkers held that the spiritual sphere should be distinguished from the temporal and that the Church was responsible for the one and the State for the other, it has never been possible to draw a clear line between them. Most concrete situations and actions involve both, and therefore involve both Church and State. It is not relevant here to discuss these controversies, nor the quarrels between Empire and Papacy or king and episcopate. What matters is the general acceptance of the belief that a man's daily life would be controlled by his religion, combined with the habit of letting his religion, and therefore his moral theory, be controlled by the official organs of the Church. If the moral achievement of the Middle Ages has been absurdly exaggerated by some Christian apologists and, in recent times, by opponents of capitalism, the grandeur of the ideal has not been sufficiently acknowledged by those who prefer to dwell on the failures in practice. On any reckoning the *Summa Theologica* of St. Thomas Aquinas is one of the greatest creations of human thought, and that not only in respect of its 'pure' theology, but also of the intellectual foundation which it furnished for a Christian society.

The bare fact that the higher clergy were ceaselessly occupied with public affairs is familiar enough. To begin with our own country, it is not merely that the bishops have always sat in the House of Lords and its predecessors. For centuries after the Norman conquest successive kings looked to the Archbishop of Canterbury, as William I had done, for political counsel. 'Hoc est consilium regis et meum,' wrote Lanfranc. 'This is the king's counsel and mine.' In the next reigns 'the Archbishop of Canterbury is still recognized as the first constitutional adviser of the Crown: William Rufus acknowledges the right of Lanfranc as distinctly as Henry I does that of Anselm '.[2] Later, the office of Chancellor, which carried with it the presidency or speakership of the House of Lords, was frequently held by the Archbishop—by Reynolds, Stratford, Langham, Arundel, Bourchier, Morton, Warham. In virtue of the high standard of education required for its proper fulfilment, this office was entrusted to a cleric, always until 1340 and thereafter usually until 1529. At first they were rewarded, like Becket, with bishoprics; subsequently—and this is the more remarkable as lay education became more common, especially among lawyers—they were chosen from among the leading bishops, such as Courtenay, Arundel, Kemp and Stafford (before they were appointed to the See of Canterbury), Beaufort and Wolsey.

The Treasurers, too, were mostly clerics and usually bishops until the fifteenth century. The even more important office of Justiciar was held by clerics until the reign of Henry II, whose predecessors found it safer to use a bishop as their chief executive minister rather than a secular lord who might succeed in making the post hereditary. Odo, Bishop of Bayeux, Ralph Flambard, later Bishop of Durham, Bloett, Bishop of Lincoln, Roger, Bishop of Salisbury, discharged this function, though not always under the same title. The last group of clerical Justiciars, Longchamp, Bishop of Ely, Walter of Coutances, Archbishop of Rouen, Hubert Walter, Archbishop of Canterbury, and Peter des Roches, Bishop of Winchester, occurs under the sons of Henry II, who (says Stubbs)

needed ministers 'qualified to act as mediators between themselves and their people '.[3] These high officers of state were
supported by a great host of clerical civil servants.

Given such a representation in the King's Council, the
'official' Church was the less likely to intervene corporately,
through synod or convocation for example, in political or
social affairs. The bishops used their influence for good or
ill within the Council or within Parliament. Though occasionally we may have record of what they said, we must in
general be content to praise or blame the national policy without expecting to disentangle the ecclesiastical contribution.
There are times, however, when the leadership of the Church
is evident and fruitful, occasionally, indeed, vital to our
national growth. The sober Stubbs indulges himself for a
moment in something like a panegyric when, at the close of
his first volume, he reviews the action of the clergy. 'They
by their vindication of their own liberties showed the nation
that other liberties might be vindicated as well, and that there
are bounds to the power and violence of princes. They had
fought the battle of the people in fighting their own. From
them too, as subjects and not merely as churchmen, the first
movements towards national action had come. They had
bound up the wounds of the perishing State at the accession
of Henry II; they had furnished the first if not the only
champions of freedom in the royal councils, where S. Thomas,
S. Hugh, and Archbishop Geoffrey had had courage to speak
where the barons were silent. . . . It was the common Church
which combined Norman and Englishman in one service, when
law and language, land tenure and political influence, would
have made them two races of lords and slaves. . . . Hubert
Walter, the administrator of Henry's system, who under
Richard and John completed the fabric of strong government
by means of law, and Stephen Langton, who deserves more
than any other person the credit of undoing the mischief that
arose from that system, maintaining the law by making the
national will the basis of the strength of government, were
both representative men of the English Church.'[4] A little

D

discounting of the future Bishop of Oxford's enthusiasm will not invalidate the substantial justice of his verdict.

In the wider field of Europe, the names of Gregory VII and Innocent III speak for the secular and political influence of the Church. When Henry IV knelt in the snow at Canossa, the priest in Gregory had to give him absolution, so that the Emperor recovered temporarily from the advantage which the Pope had held over him. But it is far from true that Gregory's victory was for this reason illusory. Canossa remained in men's memories and imaginations to symbolize the supremacy of the Church over the State. Innocent III (1198-1216), a far greater personality and statesman than any secular prince of his day, preached his consecration sermon on the text, ' See, I have this day set thee over the nations and over the kingdoms, to pluck up and to break down, and to destroy, and to overthrow; to build, and to plant.' (Jeremiah i, 10.) With him, the right of the Church to take cognisance of all sin everywhere broke through the distinction of secular and spiritual spheres. So when he tried to make peace between Philip II of France and John of England and when Philip protested that the Pope could not interfere with the feudal relation between lord and vassal, Innocent declared that he was acting ' *ratione peccati* ' [by reason of sin]. ' In his relations with the temporal powers Innocent was governed by the thought of Gregory VII: the Pope is responsible to God for the salvation of kings just as much as of ecclesiastics. It is his business to exhort them to righteousness and peaceful conduct towards each other and to respect for the rights of the Church. Much of his effort was directed to preserving among the newer or less securely based monarchies the forces of order that favoured reforming canonical ideas. Where he could, he continued the Gregorian policy of binding them to the Roman See by the feudal contract; where he could not, he intervened by remonstrance or excommunication and interdict to defend the *jus canonicum* against the conflicting claims of national custom or individual interest.'[5]   He claimed the right to approve the electoral choice of the Emperor; he placed Leon and Castile under an interdict when Alfonso IX refused to separate from Berenguela after the Pope had annulled their marriage on grounds of consanguinity; the kings of Aragon and Portugal were his feudal vassals, and John resigned the crown of England to receive his kingdom back as a papal fief. No Pope was ever so powerful again. Innocent IV developed the legal aspects of intervention *ratione peccati*; Boniface VIII even raised the papal claims, but came to grief over them. States grew stronger as the Papacy weakened. Yet the Emperor Lewis, the Bavarian, had to yield to the Avignon Pope John XXII, and it was not until after the seventeenth century that the Popes deliberately renounced this kind of political intervention.

What has just been said is intended only to illustrate the political activity and significance of the higher clergy from Pope to bishop. The moral quality and the results of their acts were far too varied to be enclosed within a few sweeping generalizations. Reserving any judgement of the results until more of the field has been surveyed, we may venture some comments on their morality, which must properly be considered in the light of their intentions. Both Gregory VII and Innocent III strove after power; and power tends to corrupt. But Gregory wanted power primarily in order to cleanse the Church itself. Only by wresting the appointment of bishops from secular hands could he freely choose men who would carry out his reforms. And in so far as he wanted power over the world (for he was led on to stake out higher claims by the course of the Investitures Controversy) he seems to have been completely sincere in his passion for righteousness. Innocent, with similar intentions, was aware that pitch defiles and could not avoid touching it. Convinced that only a strong papacy could restrain the secular powers from evil-doing, he had to make and keep it strong, especially at the centre, in Italy. Hence his self-regarding dealings with Sicily and the Empire. Again, the Pope must be master in his own house. Hence the Inquisition. The higher one's aims, the more insidious is the temptation to seek power in order to enforce them, to let the end justify the means. The temptation which Jesus conquered was often too strong for those who called themselves His vicars. But to suppose that on the whole they were pursuing power or wealth for their own sake would be monstrously unjust.

The Church and Law

It was not only—and indeed not principally—by a series of particular protests and individual interventions that the Church sought to promote the welfare of society. It exerted a continual and distinctively official pressure by means of the Canon Law. Although the majority of the canons passed by the earlier Councils of the Church dealt with ecclesiastical affairs in the restricted sense, the necessity of defining the discipline and penitential system of the Church brought many matters of conduct, particularly sexual, within the orbit of canon law. It was deemed prudent, for example, to prescribe what occupations were closed to the Christian, as when the Spanish Council of Elvira, early in the fourth century, declared that any charioteer (i.e. in races) or pantomime actor who became a Christian must renounce his profession! Legislation of this kind, while it can never have been fully effective, carried great weight so long as exclusion from the communion of the Church was sincerely dreaded. The developed canon law tried to bring as much of daily life as possible under the control of the Church. 'The ideal of the golden age of the canonists was to make a working reality of the kingdom of God upon earth; to express the laws of that kingdom in a coherent, all-embracing code, and to enforce that code upon the still half-heathen kingdoms of the world. An ideal truly, and predestined to fail; but a noble ideal.'[6] But failure to achieve all its ends was not incompatible with a great deal of influence. Fundamental to all social life is the family, and therefore the law of marriage. For some centuries this was almost wholly ecclesiastical, and was administered by Church courts. Long after the Reformation ecclesiastical influence remained powerful in England.

Much can be said against the ecclesiastical marriage laws. At some points (e.g. affinity) so strict that the necessary exceptions bred chaos, at others, especially regarding the distinction between betrothal and marriage, so uncertain as to perplex the lawyer and destroy the plain man's confidence, it was far too dependent upon the papal power of definition and dispensation, even if that power was wisely used. But the common law, preoccupied with the property aspects of marriage, had plenty of faults, while the law of the Church, with all its defects, upheld the religious ideal of a lifelong union of one man and one woman, with mutual obligations, as the essential cell of a healthy social organism. Moreover, it set its face against the exclusion of any class from full marriage; differing in this respect from Roman law, it was here creatively equalitarian. Western canon law, through its monopoly of marriage, also reduced the severity of parental control granted to the father by Roman law and Germanic custom. Family life was further affected in England by ecclesiastical control of wills. After the thirteenth century, except in boroughs, land could not be devised by will. With this important exception, Church law determined and Church courts administered the law of testamentary and intestate succession. To begin with, the parish priest usually drew up the will; it was proved and housed in diocesan or archiepiscopal registries; and any disputes were settled by ecclesiastical lawyers.

On the Continent and to a lesser extent in England the canonical legislation concerning oaths had far-reaching consequences. In Roman law, with certain exceptions, simple agreements were not legally binding. Hence men began to seek greater security in their bargains by taking oaths. The Church disliked the practice at first, but acquiesced in it, claiming in consequence to control a practice which implied an obligation towards God as well as towards man. So the canonists of the twelfth century tried to secure legal remedies for the non-fulfilment of pacts. 'At every opportunity the Church freed the law of contract from formalism, and finally declared, in spite of the Roman maxim *ex nudo pacto actio*

non oritur [no legal action arises from a bare agreement], that
a simple promise was enforceable. It must have needed a
great deal of courage to reach this position when against it was
all the authority of Roman law and the custom and practice
of most of the other systems of secular law.'[7] This canonical
use of 'good faith' was to make its mark on economic life,
particularly in certain commercial developments. Insurance
was facilitated and debts were more easily negotiable—but
the economic influence of the Church must be treated separ-
ately. Even in England, where the common lawyers developed
their own law of contract and frequently called their ecclesiastical colleagues (or rivals) to account for drawing such
matters into the Church courts, the ecclesiastical tribunals
persisted in their efforts to enforce contractual promises made
by oath or by pledges of faith.[8]

Canon law was a means by which the Church intervened
in social life officially and directly. Less direct, but by no
means unofficial, was its influence upon the common law.
The Germanic invaders of the Roman Empire brought with
them their own customary law by which they continued to
live while their Roman subjects, under the then accepted principle of the personality of law, lived by Roman law. But the
systems were not mutually impervious, and Christian ideas
were brought to bear upon the barbarians through a Chris-
tianized Roman law. Perhaps the most striking example is
the Lombardic law, thoroughly German before its reduction
to writing by King Rothari (A.D. 643) but thereby at once in-
corporating material from Roman and canon law. The process quickened under Liutprand in the following century. 'He
was the Church's main agent in the moulding of Lombard
law in conformity with the Church's law. . . . The permeation
of the code of Rothari and his successors by the rules and
principles of Canon Law shows us clearly how the Church, as
the framer and interpreter of divine law, inspires the modification of secular law to suit the precepts of divine law.'[9]

Similar development is found in England. Except for the
protection of ecclesiastical property with which they open, the

'dooms which King Ethelbert established in the lifetime of Augustine' are entirely Germanic; a century later the laws of Wihtred of Kent might almost have come from a Church Council. Observe, for example, the law prohibiting Sunday labour, an inestimable boon to a hard-working peasantry. The same provision is made in the laws of Ine of Wessex (c. 690)—'if a slave works on Sunday by his lord's command, he shall become free '—and was perpetuated by the ordinances agreed between the English and the Danes and by the laws of Athelstan.[10] Meanwhile Charlemagne had given the same royal protection to Sunday in his realms. In years to come, and especially after the Protestant reduction of ecclesiastical holidays, the toiling masses of industry were to benefit even more than the peasant from an enforced day of rest, however exaggerated its restrictions upon recreation. 'Thank God for the chap who thought of Sunday,' says a character in Thomas Armstrong's *King Cotton*.

To return to Anglo-Saxon England, Alfred's laws are predominantly Germanic and conservative, but a Christian setting to them was furnished by the introductory extracts from the Bible—the Ten Commandments, other parts of the Mosaic law, passages from the Sermon on the Mount and from the Acts of the Apostles. Further, 'there are important features in his laws which are not derived from any known source and may well be original. They include provisions protecting the weaker members of society against oppression, limiting the ancient custom of the blood-feud, and emphasizing the duty of a man to his lord. A religious king, whose own life had once depended on the loyalty of his men, might be expected to legislate in this spirit.'[11]

Upon criminal law, too, the Church's influence was considerable in introducing punishment by imprisonment, so that the offender might be brought to repentance, in calling upon the king to promote morality and not only to maintain order and custom, in teaching men to look to the king as the guardian of justice, so that offences became crimes against the state, and above all in shifting the very basis of criminal liability from the compensation of the injured party to the culpability of the individual wrong-doer. Bracton, taught by the canonists, helped to establish in English criminal justice the doctrine of guilty intention and the use of moral tests to distinguish the gravity of crimes.

The mutual influence of Canon and Civil law, usually studied together, was another channel by which the Church has affected European countries, particularly those which abandoned their customary law and formally received the civil law. Although this did not happen in England, Roman law made its impact on our common law, both directly and through the canonists, at least in the sphere of judicial machinery and procedure. As Sir William Holdsworth has written, 'During the Middle Ages, the canon law exercised a similar but a wider influence than the civil law in securing firstly the permanence of those intellectual and political ideas by which this period is distinguished; and secondly the spread of those more enlightened legal ideas upon such matters as the machinery by which the law should be administered, the form in which its rules should be expressed, and the substance of some of its rules, all of which it had inherited from its close and continuous association with the civil law.'[12]   And when the common law had so far developed that its precision and rigidity called for a supplementary system of equity, the Chancellor's court was able to introduce remedies based on the Christian and canonical conception of conscience as deciding what is moral and therefore equitable. As Cardinal Morton ruled when Chancellor, 'Every law should be in accordance with the law of God; and I know well that an executor who fraudulently misapplies goods and does not make restitution will be damned in Hell, and to remedy this is in accordance with conscience, as I understand it.'[13]

The Church and War

That war is an evil thing few will question. It has therefore been urged against the Christian Church that, so far from denouncing all wars as evil and forbidding its members to engage in them, it has usually countenanced them, the authorities in rival countries each assuring the faithful of their duty to fight and each invoking the blessing of God upon their fighting. Further, it has been widely felt that the Church, being an international society, might have stopped wars simply by forbidding its members to take part in them. These arguments need elucidation. As to the latter point, it is pertinent to recall that before 1914 many believed that the 'solidarity of the workers' would make war between civilized nations impossible. In the event, national sentiment and interest proved the stronger power. It is only too probable that a call from the Church would have produced no better result, even in the Middle Ages. At no time has Christianity secured the complete allegiance of its adherents, at no time has the Church been composed of perfect men. As has been said already, Christian social success can be properly judged (if at all) only on the basis of the Christian conception of human nature.

As to the first point, while the pacifist is bound to think the Church wrong in its refusal to endorse his position without qualification, most men, whether Christian or not, have judged that in a grievously imperfect society war is sometimes justified as the lesser evil. It ought also to be admitted that in any given case the issues are usually obscure, especially at the time of decision. Unless the moral situation is quite clear, Christians as such have no special ability to discern the balance of right and wrong. In each country they will be largely in the hands of their government, while if an international Church, like that of Rome, should attempt to pronounce where the guilt lies, the citizens of the indicted nation will probably not accept the verdict, but will upbraid the Church for 'interfering' in politics.

In fact the Church has taken the moral problem of war most seriously. Before Constantine there were some pacifists (e.g. Tertullian) and many who leaned that way (e.g. Origen, Lactantius); some of the Church Orders forbade all killing, others allowed military service. There can be no doubt that the Church was aware of the incongruity of war with the teaching of its Lord, and was worried about the application of that teaching to existing circumstances. After Constantine, when the responsibility of fighting could no longer be passed over to non-Christians, most teachers came to think that civilization as they knew it (which meant in fact the Roman Empire) ought to be defended against barbarism. This led on to consideration of the 'rules of war', notably by St. Ambrose and St. Augustine. To begin with, what is a just war? Cicero's answer, which is far from clear, appears to contemplate empire as a possible object of a just war.[14] It was an advance, there-fore, when Ambrose and Augustine ruled out conquest and aggression altogether. Self-defence they accepted, rightly or wrongly; but, anxious that this should not leave openings for a disguised selfishness, they interpreted self-defence as a form of justice, an attempt to repress the injustice of aggression. On this ground, they saw, one must go a step further. Following Cicero, they recognized that if you are prepared to defend yourself in the name of justice, you must be prepared to defend others against aggression. 'He who does not repel an injury from a fellow (*socius*) when he can, is as much at fault as he who commits the injury.'[15]

Some will think this position erroneous; some Christians, indeed, will judge that it rests more upon the teaching of Cicero than of Jesus. Still, it was an honest effort of thought (made, it should be noticed, by bishops) which, together with other aspects of Augustine's teaching, laid the foundations of the law of nations. Mere retaliation was ruled out no less than aggression. A just war must be fought by lawful authority and formally declared. Throughout, efforts must be made to secure peace. In the details of war, soldiers must behave as Christians. Augustine's maxims were incorporated through Gratian into the Canon Law and so formed the basis of all subsequent merciful, if illogical, mitigations of the horrors of war by international agreement.

Augustine's insistence on peace-making (blessed are the peace-makers, and not simply the passively peaceable) was no mere sentiment; it promoted the idea of arbitration. Where the national state is not only politically, but also, so to speak, morally sovereign, as in the ancient world, there is no machinery to enforce the notion of a just war. A universal religion embodied in a supra-national Church provides a standard of judgement and a court of reference. So, despite all the failures of Christian practice, it was a stage towards the goal to which we still stumble our way when the canon lawyers adopted the principle that no war is justifiable unless no superior tribunal is available and unless force is the only available means of vindicating justice. The Popes have not infrequently acted as arbitrators, and still more often offered their services. If it has become less likely that secular states will submit their case to any ecclesiastical court, it remains true that the cause of arbitration owes much to the Christian conscience, sometimes working through the official organs of the Church, sometimes exercising the pressure of public opinion upon governments. Serious efforts to prevent war still turn upon the definition and proclamation of aggression and the use of arbitration; and though these ideas may not be specifically Christian, it is through the Church that they have influenced European thought.[16]

Another principle and another fact must be kept in mind if the Church's teaching on war is to be judged. The principle is that war must be proportionate to its end, in other words that the good to be achieved by a war must be reasonably supposed to be greater than the certain evils which it will bring, and that no more violence should be used than is necessary to achieve this good. The fact is that both in the later Roman Empire and in the Middle Ages it seemed easier to carry a just war through to a speedy end without the enormous concurrent and consequent evils which modern wars have entailed. Perhaps we shall soon be compelled to decide, without necessarily accepting absolute pacifism, that war as we now know it cannot satisfy the conditions which the Church defined as necessary to a just war.

The power of the medieval Church as a peace-maker depended mainly upon the relation of the Pope to secular sove-

reigns. Unfortunately, from most points of view, the Pope
was himself a sovereign, with his own political interests.
Other princes were scarcely likely to trust his impartiality;
worse still, the Popes, as secular sovereigns, were frequently
engaged in war, while as Popes they promoted the Crusades,
allegedly as defensive wars. But the darker side of papal
history should not obscure the fact of numerous efforts for
international justice and peace. Gregory VII, for instance,
wrote thus to Boleslas II, Duke of Poland: 'If you really
desire these things (*sc.* peace and tranquillity), charity must
above all be observed among you: this you have violated in
the money which you have taken from the King of the
Russians. Wherefore . . . we earnestly beg and admonish
you that by the love you bear to God and St. Peter you restore
whatever has been taken from him.'[17]   Innocent II arbitrated
between England and Scotland. At the summit of papal
authority Innocent III was able to intervene beneficially at
any rate in such smaller kingdoms as Portugal, Aragon,
Poland, Armenia, Bulgaria and Serbia. In 1204 he tried to
stop war between England and France and sent three abbots
to the French king 'exhorting you in the Lord and binding
you for the remission of your fault that you make a sure peace
with the aforesaid king or enter into suitable truces that, while
permanent peace in accord with the rights of both is being
arranged between you both, you may treat more freely and
safely.'[18]   In 1235 Genoa and Venice undertook to submit
their quarrels to papal arbitration. At the end of the century
the complex relations between Boniface VIII and the kings
of France and England illustrate at once the possibility of such
arbitration and the obstacles it had to face in the Pope's own
quest for power and in national pride and selfishness, complicated by feudal law. Boniface's intervention between England
and Scotland secured a truce but could not finally avert war.
On another occasion Philip IV of France set up feudal rights
as a bar to papal intervention on moral grounds, just as his
predecessor Philip II had done with Innocent III. But was
there to be no way out of the incessant warfare bred by the

feudal system? When Guy of Flanders appealed to Rome in 1297 against his feudal superior, the King of France, 'there was a pathetic indication of the real need felt by Europe for arbitration, for some source of law above the feudal framework: here is some explanation of Rome's power, some justification perhaps of Boniface's hopes'. In August 1297 Boniface called upon France and England to make peace. The two kings were not unwilling that the papal legate should negotiate a truce, after which Rome now became a general conference ground for Europe. 'We have always thought,' said Edward, 'that the causes of the war between the King of France and ourselves should be treated of before the most Holy Father.' 'On account of the special affection which we bear to the supreme pontiff,' wrote Philip, 'we are sending plenipotentiaries to Rome.'[19] As a result a reasonable settlement was arrived at, ushering in some forty years of substantial peace between the two countries.

Although, with the waning of papal power and the divisions of the Church, it became much harder to make ecclesiastical intervention effective in politics, offers of arbitration have continued. The story somewhat resembles that of the League of Nations, unable to prevent clashes between the more powerful states or to make them conform their policies to justice, but undoubtedly useful in settling minor disputes, as when the arbitration of Cardinal Aldobrandini ended the controversy between France and Savoy over the Margravate of Saluzzo (1601) or the Nuncio Macchi dealt with the frontier question between Peru and Ecuador (1893).[20]

More picturesque, if less important in principle, was the establishment of the Peace of God and the Truce of God in the tenth century. They were the product of baronial war and were most prominent where royal control was weak. Elsewhere it remained the duty of the sovereign to suppress internal conflict.

Within France, under a feeble monarchy, there was substantial private warfare in 954, 955, 956, 957 and 958; not a prolongation of the same quarrel, but a series of distinct wars.

It was not enough to proclaim these wars unjust or to denounce as murder the feuds which customary law sanctioned, against the canon law. So, since the papacy was then at its weakest, the bishops took the lead. The movement had taken shape by A.D. 989 when a council was held at Charroux in Aquitaine, followed by others at Narbonne and Puy in 990. At the synod Guy of Anjou, Bishop of Puy, not only secured a charter of peace which threatened spiritual sanctions against those who plundered the Church, the peasantry and the merchants, but also (by a show of force, after their first refusal!) induced the knights of the neighbourhood to engage themselves under oath to observe these restrictions upon their taste for fighting. Many other bishops and some princes followed this lead, and soon other measures were approved. At the Council of Poitiers (1000) methods of arbitration were adopted to prevent outbreaks; at the Council of Bourges (1038) the Archbishop placed all males of fifteen and upwards under oath to take up arms against the disturbers of peace. Similar ecclesiastically sponsored police associations sprang up rapidly in other parts and had some measure of success until the stronger central control of the twelfth century resumed a function which properly belongs to the State.

Meanwhile a movement parallel to the leagues of the Peace of God appeared in the Truce of God. While the former sought mainly to protect the masses of the people during the operations of the feudal soldiery, the latter provided regular truces grounded in religious duties. They began in the County of Roussillon in 1027 when a synod at Toulouges forbade fighting on Sundays. More influential was a synodical letter written by bishops of the province of Arles at the suggestion of Abbot Odilo of Cluny which required a Truce of God every Thursday (the day of Christ's Ascension), Friday (His Passion), Saturday (His Burial), and Sunday (His Resurrection). The project spread quickly throughout France and was linked with the Peace of God at the Council of Narbonne (1054). Thereafter the institutions of peace were taken up in other countries, reinforced by the commendation of Pope

Urban II at the Council of Clermont (1095). To-day the idea seems fantastic, though there were occasional Christmas Day truces in the war of 1914-1918. In the eleventh century also, intentions were far better than the results. In an ecclesiastical movement the sanctions could only be ecclesiastical, namely excommunication, and this, so powerful in earlier days, was cheapened by excessive use. Nevertheless, the effort was by no means negligible. The movement remains a striking example of the Church trying ' to do something about it '. In so far as it failed, the failure underlines the truth that good societies depend upon good men.

Let the Church be blamed, and first by its own members, wherever it makes no effort to prevent war or to lay bare the causes of war. But if men organized in secular societies drag themselves into war because they *will* not hear the Gospel, that is not the fault of the Church. Moreover, the naïve longing for God to prevent war by direct intervention, and the argument that He does not exist or is not Love because He does not so intervene, rests on a radical misapprehension of the Christian understanding of God. Though, in a profounder sense, He is always intervening to prevent war and other evils, He does not put things right by mere fiat, thus reducing men to the status of puppets. War will not be conquered by a miraculous act of God nor at the behest of some sovereign Church, but by obedience to that word and will of God which the Church inadequately but unceasingly proclaims.

The Church and Economic Life

A healthy economic system depends partly upon the technical skill of economists and business men and partly upon the probity of all organizers, producers, middlemen and consumers. With the first the Church has little to do : the second is one of its most obvious concerns. How its moral responsibility is to be discharged must vary according to the status and effective influence of the Church in a particular society. Sometimes it will be looked to for theological opinions on matters properly technical—a dangerous situation—and sometimes the economist will take up the dogmatic rôle, even to the point of excluding morality from his 'laws'. Three duties, at any rate, must be discharged by the Church. It must prophesy against injustice, as Amos and Isaiah prophesied; it must help ordinary people to act honourably and charitably; and it must work out the theological and moral foundations of economics, together with a theological critique, where applicable, of current economic doctrine.

The medieval Church had opportunities since closed, for economic theory had scarcely been distinguished from ethics and most theorists were clerics. Broadly speaking, two lines of thought were possible, one leading to withdrawal from ordinary economic life, the other pervading it with Christian ideas. In the first case, the note of renunciation would be struck and material things disparaged, a mood which appears at its gentlest and sweetest in St. Francis but could take a dualist form, as in the early Manichaean heresy or in the thirteenth-century Catharist movement[21] so fiercely suppressed by Innocent III. A recurrent, if rarely achieved, object of monasticism was to experiment with social organization outside the main stream of economic life and so, it was hoped, to set up a community more capable of expressing the higher Christian virtues.

However, the second type of thought predominated. The Church tried to baptize the life of the whole community. Fundamental to this endeavour was the conception of society as a single organism, a body with many members, each with a duty to all, each with rights emerging from its duties. No doubt the class structure of feudal society was too readily accepted as immutable, but, on that premise, the Church demanded the performance of its duties from each class and thereby protected the rights of each class. At this stage it championed liberties rather than liberty.

The paramount social duty of the majority was to work. It may not be understood how much we owe to the biblical doctrine of work. Always men have had to work, but very different ideas have been associated with the necessity. The

Indian religious classics, for example, have little or nothing to say of it. The Greeks set up the ideal of the cultured gentleman with leisure to engage in the affairs of his city, in the arts and in intellectual pursuits. Prolonged labour would be detrimental to such a man's development. Conversely, Aristotle cannot think of the craftsman or labourer as truly part of the state, since they do not rule. Agricultural work was respectable, as being at least good for the body. Of black-coated occupations Xenophon says that cities should rate them low ' for they injure the bodies of those who spend their time on them by compelling them to remain indoors and sedentary, and sometimes even to spend all day by the fire! ' The crafts-man who made things himself was tolerated, perhaps re-spected, partly through Greek love of the arts, but also because he could take time off to go to the assembly or the theatre when he felt like it. Retail trade was looked down on both for its preoccupation with money-making and because the shop-keeper stays indoors. ' In well-ordered states,' said Plato, ' they are commonly those who are weakest in bodily strength and therefore of little use for any other purpose. No one will earn his living that way if he can help it.' Sheer labouring work and all dirty work, though out of doors and calling for bodily strength, was thoroughly despised and, if done at all, was turned over to slaves.

Against this attitude the Cynics and some of the later Stoics taught that work is good. Rome, however, inherited this ' gentlemanly ' outlook (witness Cicero) which has influenced the social thought of Europe, begetting various snobberies. It contains certain truths—the value of leisure for intellectual, æsthetic and physical development, the call to take part in public duties—but it needed refashioning after a Christian model with much more emphasis on the duty to work for the common good.

The Bible begins with a God who works, a scandal to mature Greek thought, if congenial to its earlier myths. Man, then, who is made in the image of God, must be a worker by nature. ' Six days shalt thou labour.' God blesses ' the work

E

of thy hands' and puts His spirit into Bezaleel 'in all manner of workmanship'. The Proverbs inveigh against the sluggard and Ecclesiasticus, not without touches of the Greek spirit, praises the farmer, the smith, the potter and every artificer. 'Without these shall not a city be inhabited. . . . They will maintain the fabric of the world; and in the handywork of their craft is their prayer.' It is said that every Jewish boy, however wealthy his family, was taught a trade; and the workman's shop at Nazareth has for ever sanctified the labour of the hands. It is a mistake to suppose that Christianity thinks of work as a legacy of the Fall. From the beginning God 'took the man and put him into the garden of Eden to dress and to keep it'. (Gen. i; Exod. xx, 9; xxxv, 30-5; Proverbs vi, 6; Ecclus. xxxviii; Gen. ii, 15.) As the Fathers taught, with perfect truth, the sin of man has increased the sweat and the toil; but work in itself is proper to the nature of man and necessary to his dignity and spiritual health, as the unemployed knew only too well between the wars.

What the Germanic barbarians thought about work is not clear. In so far as they were conquerors, living on their conquests, the general equivalence of worker and conquered or slave probably suggested the indignity of labour. The Christian idea of work was one of the lessons a convert had to learn. In this respect they were set an example by the Benedictine monks whose rule demanded labour and who taught many skilled crafts. To cut a long and highly interesting story short, medieval society accepted the moral obligation of work and the doctrine that rights or privileges are grounded in the fulfilment of the obligations of one's station.

'One's station' was a notion too easily accepted and too statically interpreted, as has been admitted, though, paradoxically enough, the most rapid and most democratic promotion was possible in the Church itself. While it cannot be denied that the medieval Church thought more of order than of liberty, we must remember how hard it had struggled to bring the precious order out of chaos. And so Pope and canonist, bishop and parish priest, preached content with one's lot, however lowly in this world. As agricultural life was settled and orderly enough, attention was directed to the avarice which breeds discontent, which piles up the riches which dislocate the *status quo*. In practice, that meant an attempt to regulate industry and especially trade. Since it is impossible to survey the whole field here, a word must be said about the gilds, the just price and usury.

The gilds have been belauded beyond their deserts by romantic medievalists of the Bellocian order. Most of the religious gilds had nothing to do with industry, and many of those which had some connection with it were not more than friendly societies (for which the Church may take some credit). The comparatively few men who ever belonged to a craft gild joined it for economic, not religious, reasons. The religious attributes and associations of the gilds did indeed serve the excellent purpose of reminding the craftsmen that their daily work was to be connected with their faith and worship; but only too often the gilds used the form of a religious association for selfish ends. At bottom, they existed to preserve monopolies. However, granted the principle of monopoly, they were economically and in some ways morally valuable. Standards of workmanship were maintained, wages and prices were fixed. At this point in particular the Church made itself felt by its doctrine of the Just Price.

Caveat emptor, said Roman Law, the buyer must look after his own interests; and Christianity flatly contradicted it. In towns, foodstuffs were a matter for the municipal authorities. The consumer was protected by the enforced practice of open markets, with middlemen reduced to a minimum. City edicts, with the support of the Church, forbade forestalling and regrating (buying goods from the producer before they reached the market or buying in the market to resell at a higher price) and engrossing (cornering goods to dominate prices). But manufactured articles, being monopoly products, needed a different treatment; and so the gilds were used to enforce the current doctrine of the just price, which St. Thomas Aquinas based on the golden rule, 'Do unto others as you would they should do unto you.' More specifically, he advocated a price determined by the cost of materials and labour, with some allowance for scarcity. Supply and demand were to be factors, but not the only or over-riding factors, in price-fixing; 'the bugbear is the man who uses, or even creates, a temporary shortage, the man who makes money out of the turn of the market, the man who, as Wyclif says, *must* be wicked, or he could not have been poor yesterday and rich to-day '.[22]

Small-scale manufacture, direct relations between producer and consumer, and a habit of allowing authority to restrain liberty for the common good facilitated the application of this doctrine. But as industry and commerce grew, the system creaked, the theologians made more concessions to subjective valuation and began to entertain the possibility that a fair price is best reached by free contract. If our question is whether the Church tried to help society, the correctness and practicability of just price theories is less significant than the underlying belief that there can be such a thing and the tenacious endeavour to subordinate economic practice to moral considerations.

The commercial development which so much complicated the theory of a just price upset still more completely the ancient ecclesiastical objection to usury. While the early Church, like Aristotle, had been unsympathetic to trade, its legitimacy had to be recognized. Although there was much prejudice against the non-producer, the man who merely bought to sell at a profit, the importance of the middleman's services came gradually to be appreciated, until Aquinas could write that trade (*negotiatio*) is unobjectionable when it is undertaken for the common good (*propter publicam necessitatem*) and when the profit is sought not as an end in itself, but as a wage paid for labour.

Large-scale industry and commerce cannot be carried on without capital. Should capital earn interest? The Church had combined a few biblical texts, notably the *Mutuum date nihil inde sperantes* of Luke vi, 35,[23] with Aristotle's teaching that money is barren, that is, a mere means of exchange, not

a commodity and not in itself productive. The law of nature,
it was believed, joined itself to biblical and philosophical
authority, for to live on interest is to live without working.
Usury, therefore (which meant interest as such, not extortionate interest), had been forbidden to the clergy from very
early times, while from the ninth century the prohibition had
extended to the laity and cases of usury were brought within
the jurisdiction of the ecclesiastical courts. This outlook fitted
well enough into an economic background when comparatively
little money was used by private persons and when loans were
not so much required for capital transactions as for immediate
consumption. Mostly they were to meet personal distress; and
a Christian should not profit from the troubles of his neighbour, but freely help him. But as capital loans became
familiar, it had to be conceded that money so used is productive and that interest may be earned at least where risk
is shared. Fixed interest charges without partnership in risk
were still opposed. Other relaxations were found expedient
until theologians and canonists together, by such devices as
compensation to the lender for cessation of gain while his
money is not in his possession, had worked out a rough distinction between interest and usury and had adapted the law
of the Church to the new economic situation. Probably the
control of usury did not amount to much after the twelfth or
thirteenth century. Still, the attempt kept alive the all-
important principle that business transactions must be morally
justifiable. 'Business is business' had not yet been erected
into a law of nature.

The spirit of medieval economic teaching has been well
summarized by Troeltsch: 'Property and gain are based upon
the personal performance of work; goods are exchanged only
when necessary, and then only according to the principles of
a just price, which does not give an undue advantage to anyone (this just price is best regulated by the government); consumption is regulated (*a*) in accordance with the principle of
moderation, which only permits the natural purpose of the
maintenance of existence to be fulfilled, and (*b*) which makes

room for a generosity which takes the needs of others into account; at the same time great differences in social position and in fortune, and therefore in the exercise of liberality, are fully recognized.'[24] This system, calling for so much self-restraint, 'can only really be produced with the aid of the Christian virtues of love, humility, and hope—a hope which is anchored in the real values of the future life.'

Only too often the Church was faithless to its own precepts. *Corruptio optimi pessima.* (That which has the most power for good can produce the greatest evil if it is misused, e.g. atomic energy.) Yet it is impossible to believe that medieval society would have been better without the measure of inspiration which it drew from its teachers and the measure of control which even a semi-Christian public opinion enforced.

Some Examples of Christian Influence

A more comprehensive study of the impact of Christianity upon medieval life would have to take into account several institutions which the Church cannot claim as its own but which would have fared badly without its support or which were adopted by it as instruments of civilization. Universities are an example of the first class, chivalry of the second.

The transmutation of the mere fact of knighthood (probably Germanic in origin) into the half-religious, half-romantic ideal of chivalry may be regarded as a sequel to efforts to protect the unwarlike by the Peace and Truce of God. In both cases it was taken for granted that knights and their retainers could not be kept altogether quiet. The institutions of peace, therefore, tried to hedge the fighting off from certain classes, while chivalry was intended to sublimate pride and pugnacity, especially in association with the Crusades. Among the good results must be reckoned the sense that courage and military prowess ought to be the means of serving one's fellows, the obligation to protect the distressed, courtesy, fidelity to the word of a knight, the training of boys in chivalrous ways, and certain elementary laws of war, tempering sheer brutality by the recognition of an international fraternity. A strange medley, with some strange and unhappy consequences, it was nevertheless a means by which Christian ideals got some hold upon a difficult section of humanity.

Universities were not as such the creation of the Church. In Italy, where some tradition of lay education had lingered, the earliest universities were the schools of law and medicine at Bologna and Salerno. In Northern Europe, however, the centres of learning after Charlemagne's Palace School were the monasteries, and later on the cathedral schools which rose to a particular prominence as part of the twelfth century renaissance; Chartres and Paris are outstanding examples. It was in the schools belonging to Notre Dame, the cathedral church of Paris, that Abelard taught, and out of these schools that the University of Paris grew up to be a fruitful mother of children. Though they paid some attention to law and medicine, these northern universities were distinguished by their study of theology and philosophy. That their scholars were technically clerics is no proof of ecclesiastical support, which is to be seen rather in patronage, benefactions and above all in the supply of teachers, particularly the great Dominican and Franciscan friars. As an international body, the Church was also in a position to sanction the authority to confer degrees, which conveyed the right to teach in all countries; most universities received a papal charter. Further, whereas many continental universities were established by princes, the collegiate system which has played so great a part in English higher education owes much to ecclesiastical enterprise. William, Archdeacon of Durham, gave Oxford its first income from investment, out of which University College was eventually founded; Merton, the first college to receive a formal constitution and detailed statutes, was founded by Walter Merton, afterwards Bishop of Rochester; all the surviving medieval colleges of Oxford except Balliol were founded by ecclesiastics (mostly bishops); and the one exception owes its origin to the penalty imposed upon John Balliol by the Bishop of Durham. Peterhouse, the first Cambridge college, was established by Hugh, Bishop of Ely, after the Merton model which also influenced the Parisian college of Navarre. Meanwhile the greater part of pre-university education was carried out by the Church—monastic schools, cathedral schools, Latin or Grammar schools and elementary parish schools. Only towards the close of the Middle Ages do lay foundations become at all common.

Modern objections to 'charity' have two excellent grounds, first the fear of sapping individual responsibility and of creating a pauperized or mendicant class, and secondly the danger of multiplying palliatives instead of removing radical evils in the social structure. As to the first point, it would require much detailed study before one could fairly assess the responsibility of the Church. The example of the *Didascalia* (p. 20) shows early ecclesiastical awareness of the problem, and is not at all exceptional; on the other hand it has been alleged, probably with truth, that monastic charity scarcely fed the poor which it created. Deeper than any blindness or negligence, the prudent administration of charity is crossed, for the Christian, by the knowledge that even those whom men count worthless must be helped, since the charity of God Himself is rained upon the just and the unjust. In any case, it is fair to point out that the State has found the problems of poor relief no less difficult to solve from the sixteenth century, when it so largely took the matter out of the hands of the Church, until to-day.

To the second charge the Church must to a considerable extent plead guilty, entering at the same time a reasonable plea of extenuating circumstances in that the sheer necessity of order was so great, during the centuries when the Church had the most direct social power, as to obscure the parallel need for change and progress. But given that the Church, rightly or wrongly, saw the preservation of social order as a duty and therefore taught the individual to acquiesce in restraints upon his liberty and in material poverty in order to do the duties of his station, the charitable activities of the Church cannot be classed as bits and pieces of palliation; rather, charity on a big scale was part of the social system.

At the very least, the official Church deserves a great deal of gratitude for inventing and experimenting in those social services which all modern governments find necessary. Education was one, hospitals another. The variety, as well as the number, of hospitals founded by the Christian Church in the fourth and fifth centuries (cf. p. 36) was increased in later days by the foundation of hospitals for the insane, houses for converted Jews and for poor clergy. In the North Riding of Yorkshire there is record of ninety-one medieval hospitals, while the Almoner of Durham Cathedral Priory maintained four in the small city of Durham and its immediate vicinity. Small as many of them were, the aggregate is impressive.

As it is sometimes affirmed that the Church rarely protests against existing institutions, two interesting examples of successful action deserve attention. Trial by ordeal of fire or water, a common practice in primitive societies, was deeply rooted in the Germanic nations among which Christianity spread. The Church was divided upon its use. In the sixth century Avitus, Bishop of Vienne, objected to wager of battle, Agobard, Bishop of Lyons, wrote against ordeals in the ninth century, and they were forbidden by Popes Leo IV, Stephen V and Sylvester II. The custom was approved, however, by a number of councils from the ninth century to the eleventh and by such eminent ecclesiastics as Hincmar, Archbishop of Rheims, and the canonist Ivo of Chartres. This being the predominant opinion, the Church for a time sought to strengthen the ordeal by clothing it with religious forms. Meanwhile the alternative method of wager at law or compurgation was encouraged by the place given to it in the ecclesiastical courts, the emphasis laid upon the sin of perjury having a good deal of weight. For though one guilty man might commit perjury, it was less likely that he would find twelve neighbours ready to do likewise in a small society where little could remain hidden. Finally, at the Lateran Council of A.D. 1215, the clergy were forbidden to perform any religious ceremonies in connection with the ordeal. Robbed of its religious sanction, the process was useless, as Henry III at once recognized in

England. The lawyers were forced to develop new methods of deciding criminal guilt. In the words of Sir William Holdsworth, 'The ordeal was abolished at the bidding of the church, and it was this act of obedience which was one of the causes which made for the growth of the jury.'[25]

The second instance is the tournament, which comes into prominence in the eleventh century. These military sports were then so dangerous to life that the Church frequently condemned them. Papal bulls excommunicated those who took part, while Christian burial was denied to men who fell in them by the Lateran Council of 1179. Though they were too popular to be suppressed, royal ordinances so far responded to ecclesiastical complaints as to lay down conditions which removed much of the danger.

Behind such official action and far more important was the work of Christian individuals, whether great names like St. Dunstan or Abbot Suger or Louis IX in politics, St. Bernard or St. Francis leading spiritual revivals, bishops like Hugh of Lincoln and Robert Grossetete, or those Christians who best served their Church by condemning its ways, a Wycliffe, a Huss, a Savonarola, or the host of forgotten men and women who tried to live the Christian life. These were the fittest instruments by which Christ in His Church intervened in medieval society; and much of the finest energy of the Church was properly absorbed in increasing their number. There were the home missions, as when the friars at their best reinforced the parochial system in growing towns, and there were the foreign missions which brought country after country under some degree of Christian influence. It was not without mighty labours that the Northmen and the Slavs were converted in these middle centuries.[26]

In the ninth century Anskar preached heroically in both Denmark and Sweden. There was afterwards decline, recovery and more decline in Denmark before the country became substantially Christian under Canute, about A.D. 1020. In Sweden Anskar's work was destroyed, except as an inspiration, to be renewed in the eleventh century by a largely English mission and brought to fruition in the twelfth. The Northmen of Normandy accepted baptism in A.D. 911—a nominal mass-conversion which turned to enthusiasm with a quite surprising rapidity. In Norway Christianity was fairly well planted by A.D. 1000, again with much English help, and thence it spread to Iceland and Greenland. Once more there was reaction, and a reconversion under St. Olaf. Farther East, Cyril and Methodius took Christianity to Moravia in the ninth century, during which the Bulgars and Serbs also were converted; Russia and Poland followed in the tenth century, Hungary in the eleventh, Prussia and the Wends in the twelfth and thirteenth, the Baltic lands not till the fifteenth. We know far too few details of this missionary epic which laid the foundations of civilization in so much of Europe and helped to balance the losses inflicted upon Christendom by the sword of Islam. India and China, too, were touched, not yet with lasting success, while the bright spirit and original mind of Ramon Lull[27] penetrated into Islam itself.

Finally, though it is not the subject of this book, a moment's tribute is due to Christian inspiration of the arts — the cathedrals of Durham and Chartres, the Lindisfarne Gospels and the triumphs of thirteenth-century book-making, the ivories and enamels, the textiles, sculpture in wood and stone, the beginnings of polyphonic music, and the *Divina Commedia*.

The Abuse of Ecclesiastical Power

There was a bad side, of course, which must not be concealed though it cannot be described here in detail. Some of it was sheer wickedness, made more terrible by the possession of power. Popes could engage in warfare for purely temporal ends; bishops and monasteries used their influence to amass wealth; the rule of clerical celibacy did not promote sexual morality.

Other evils might have been avoided if the officers of the Church had been *less* involved in secular affairs. First, it was almost automatic for educated men, other than common lawyers, to take at least minor orders, and many of these clerics had no vocation whatsoever to the Christian ministry. They were qualifying themselves for administrative posts. The good name of the Church would have suffered less if these administrative careers had not so often been rewarded by the wealthiest rectories and by bishoprics. Secondly, even conscientious bishops, called upon to take such a full part in affairs of state, were compelled to neglect their dioceses and their proper ecclesiastical functions, or at best to discharge them through vicar-generals and other officials. A medieval prelate can rarely have been a Father in God to his clergy.

Then there were the many ways in which the official Church acted out of good motives but stooped to unworthy means. As we have seen in the cases of Gregory VII and Innocent III, an honest determination to reform the Church itself and to make the whole of society Christian drew the Popes into intermittent warfare with secular powers, since, so it was believed, they must be able to deal with kings as one powerful territorial sovereign with another and must secure to the Church freedom to appoint its bishops. But it was demoralizing to fight the world with its own weapons. The worst manifestation of good intentions perverted was the forcible suppression of heresy, and often of truth, out of zeal for orthodoxy. Presumably the good motives of the Inquisition must be granted, in the main, for it was universally believed that heresy would both deprive individual souls of eternal salvation and also destroy the foundations of society; but the means used are beyond justification, and the positive value of freedom was disregarded. Less blameworthy, but often harmful, was that authoritarian spirit or grandmotherly meddlesomeness which, unable to forget the days when it had been almost true, supposed that nothing could go right unless it was ecclesiastically controlled; a very different proposition from the requirement that every activity should be religiously and morally controlled. Workable in a simple society, this supervision broke down intellectually and technically, not to speak of the moral temptations which it offered to those who worked the machinery of control. One can see a movement against it in English constitutional history when, in 1340, Sir Robert Bourchier became the first lay Chancellor and a judge was appointed Treasurer; and again in 1371 when Edward III was petitioned to appoint laymen only to the office of chancellor, treasurer, clerk of the privy seal, baron or controller of the exchequer, or to posts of similar importance. It may be seen in the useful jealousy of English common lawyers and in the pressure brought by merchants against the canonical prohibition of usury. It burst out into a torrent in the Renaissance.

Simultaneous with this chafing against ecclesiastical controls was the denunciation of worldliness and immorality—Wycliffe, Piers Plowman and all the long tale of anti-clerical satire. The contrast between theory and practice was too glaring. And worse, the true root of Christianity was being torn up by the elaboration of ecclesiastical machinery and its financial requirements. So often the Church must have resembled a business concern which sold its wares—grace, forgiveness, salvation—for cash. Too few pious works sprang from spontaneous charity. Critic and satirist give a distorted picture of a Church which had not lost the capacity for reform, but there was reason enough for a Reformation centred upon the doctrine of Justification by Faith.

Renaissance and Reformation

Politics

TO put 'Renaissance man' into a few pages is to ask for trouble, since part of the charm of the Renaissance, part of its essence, is variety, exuberance, fertility. A few characteristics perhaps allow of generalization. As an ideal, freedom replaced authority, self-restraint yielded to self-fulfilment, stability to movement, community to independence. Man, free in mind and will, was to be autonomous. If he must acknowledge any authority, it should not be the Church. The pagan classics might furnish a pattern of life, an arbiter of taste; free associations for the cultivation of art or learning or business should be his social unit; and if coercion could not be banished from human history, it should be exercised by the man-made State.

If Renaissance thought was not always anti-Christian, it was thoroughly anti-clerical; and although the majority consciously desired no more than to escape from ecclesiastical dogmatism and dictation, it was all too easy to slip from priest-baiting into scepticism. North of the Alps, wherever priestly domination was diminished, there was less temptation to throw off the authority of God with that of the clergy. The Reformation, it has been said, *was* the Northern Renaissance. In Italy, however, man seemed to have come into his own. Humanism, even when not deliberately irreligious, set man in the centre of the universe, repudiating the limitations of creatureliness and sin and assuming that the complete development of every human faculty could be achieved without humility and without the grace of God. There is something paradoxical in the working-out of the humanist ideal. The full development of human personality turns upon the integration of many capacities, corresponding in the individual to that wholeness of society which the medieval Church had cherished. In fact, humanism led on to those autonomies of 'disinterested science', 'art for art's sake', 'pure (!) politics' and 'business is business', which dissolve the ultimate spiritual harmonies and disrupt the organic unity both of the individual and of society. The irreligious humanist is undeveloped: he is incomplete not simply because he lacks *one* element in the spiritual life, but because he has no unifying principle. Neither has the society which he creates, until in despair it allows the totalitarian State to usurp the place of religion.

It is a commonplace of modern Christian apologetic to attribute to Renaissance humanism a boundless and superficial optimism from which, in due course, the idea of inevitable progress was derived. If Machiavelli is not wholly exceptional, this is but a half-truth. To him, human depravity is axiomatic. 'Men never do good except through necessity.' He was analysing a concrete situation in which religion was being widely discounted, and his prognosis is less optimistic than the Christian, which admits the depravity but believes in the sanctifying grace of the Holy Spirit of God. Well aware that unlimited self-culture must produce an intolerable social chaos, Machiavelli found the necessary curb not in religion (though this might help where it was accepted), but in law backed by an adequate coercive power. This law would not be Christian law or natural law or any universal moral law, but positive law, man-made utilitarian enactments imposed upon the subject by the sovereign. The primary duty of the sovereign—probably but not necessarily a monarch—was to be efficient. Moreover, since positive law is *ex hypothesi* the law of a single state, the relations between states cannot be governed by law; they are left to self-interest and force. To Machiavelli, then, it was the State rather than the individual which might indulge in unbridled self-development, heedless of the rights of others and restricted only by their power.

Absolutist tendencies were strengthened also by the replacement of Common law by Roman law in several continental countries and by the alliance between monarchy and rising middle class against the nobility. On top of this came the Reformers' loyalty to the biblical doctrine of obedience to the State (Rom. xiii, I Peter ii) and their confidence in the godly prince, the divinely appointed instrument of reform. In the three main blocks of Reformed Churches, Lutheran, Calvinist and Anglican, there are considerable differences of emphasis, temperament and ultimate results, but common principles. Though each is thinking in terms of the single State instead of Christendom, none of them had yet abandoned the medieval conception of Church and State as twin aspects of one society with two sets of ministers, lay and spiritual. To them all, society is fundamentally religious and politics subordinate to morals. They were all sufficiently medieval to believe that the magistrate ought to listen to the Church, though each had its own way of dealing with the difficulties that arise in practice.

Though Luther was in some respects the most conservative of the great reformers, Calvinism was the more medieval in its political outlook. Discipline is a mark of the true Church; the ministers must scrutinize the conduct of all the members, the magistrates included, imposing spiritual penalties up to excommunication. The magistrates in their turn are bound to assist the Church in promoting moral welfare; where necessary they must add civil to the ecclesiastical penalties. In Geneva itself the discipline was exercised by the Consistory, properly an ecclesiastical court composed of the ministers and twelve elders, but presided over by one of the Syndics of the city. Civilization has known no more whole-hearted attempt to control a community's morals and manners, from the gravest crimes down to bad language or over-eating. It was much more meddlesome than the confessional, for offenders were watched for and delated to it. Wielding a power too great for any but the rarest and truest Christians, in ordinary human hands it was perilously like an ecclesiastical police-state, and one is not surprised at its unpopularity. Yet it was a most serious and sustained effort to make a community Christian. Contemporaries, at any rate, wondered at the godly city. Here is a single example of clerical persistence. The public wash-houses were no better than houses of ill fame. 'On January 25th, 1543, the Consistory appealed to the Council to stop the practice of men and women having their baths together on account of the improprieties to which this gave rise, and on March 5th it was ordered that the practice should cease. In 1548, and again in 1549, the preachers again complained, and the Council issued further instructions. But it was not until 1555, when the attention of the Council had been drawn to this matter for the fourth time, that they took practical steps to prevent its recurrence, by the simple expedient of ordering that the baths at one end of the town should be used by the men and those at the other by the women.'[1]

Luther's political teaching cannot easily be reduced to a system. One is tempted to draw up a list of the oppositions which he suggests, and then to make too much of them. There are two kingdoms, of Christ and of the world; two earthly authorities, preacher and prince; two laws, Christian and natural; two aspects of the individual, his person and his office. The temptation is to take the first member of each pair and from them to construct Luther's conception of the religious life, supposing that the rest is merely secular. Such a dualism would not be a fair interpretation of Luther. It is true that he sets great store, and rightly, upon the individual experience of that Kingdom of God which is *within* us. This is the Christian life of repentance and forgiveness, faith and grace. Herein the Christian person has liberty and joy; here the Sermon on the Mount rules. It is true also that he brings out, again quite rightly, the impossibility of applying the categories of this Christian life directly and without qualification to the life of the State as it is, in which the prince or any other man, according to his calling, will often have to act by the standards of natural law. In this order the Christian will not be able to live by the freedom with which Christ has set us free; he will get more suffering than joy. Yet as a citizen he will be serving God faithfully within the limits of circumstances which, in the last resort, are God's own responsibility. It may be that Luther

F

is more successful in distinguishing the work of parson and prince than in his most forthright utterances about the relation of Christian law (or Gospel) to natural law. But his dualism is not absolute. He makes no ultimate separation of sacred from secular and certainly does not emancipate the State from God. In practice, no one could be more anxious than Luther that the Christian conscience should operate in society. If there are spheres of conduct in which the Christian must live by the full Gospel, the law of love, and other spheres in which this is not yet possible, the point of Luther's own teaching is precisely that the Christian cannot contract out of the latter. He *must* fulfil his secular office. If it is true that German Lutherans have succumbed too often to State authority, and if, as may be true, the isolation of some elements in Luther's teaching is part cause of this, the result would probably not have come about but for other causes in German character and history, notably, it has been argued, the Thirty Years War.[2]

Anglican political theory was not unlike Luther's. The difference lay in practice, perhaps in national ethos. There was the same insistence upon obedience to the head of the State, the same confidence in the action of the layman under the godly prince, the same conception of the one body with two sets of officers. On the other hand, while the heights and depths of Luther's perception of the Gospel may have escaped all but a few, there was probably a more widely distributed political sense, a greater interest in the ways and means of applying ethics to politics and more persistence in putting pressure on the prince. Part of the theory is classically expressed by Hooker. 'We hold that seeing there is not any man of the Church of England but the same man is also a member of the commonwealth, nor any member of the commonwealth which is not also of the Church of England . . . so albeit properties and action of one do cause the name of a commonwealth, qualities and functions of another sort the name of the Church, to be given to a multitude, yet one and the selfsame multitude may in such sort be both . . .

The Church and the commonweal are in this case therefore personally one society, which society being termed a commonweal as it liveth under whatsoever form of secular law and regiment, a Church as it liveth under the spiritual law of Christ; forasmuch as these two laws contain so many and different offices, there must of necessity be appointed in it some to one charge, and some to another, yet without dividing the whole and making it two several impaled societies.' Hooker's attitude to monarchy, however, is much more constitutional than the absolutism of the mid-sixteenth century. ' So is the power of the king over all and in all limited that unto all his proceedings the law itself is a rule.' Law rests upon consent, and the commonwealth must not 'clean resign up herself and make over this power wholly into the hands of anyone '.[3]

Luther, Calvin and Hooker, then, speak of a Christian community. In so far as godliness can be procured or promoted by legislation and administration, that will be the function of the State, whether through the godly prince himself, as in most Lutheran and early Anglican teaching, or through the City Council of Calvin, or by the King in Council or Parliament as in Hooker. The spirit is still ' medieval ', though the characteristic medieval machinery associated with Pope, canon law, ecclesiastical court and confessional has disappeared or begun to lose its authority. Calvinism preserved something like the medieval machinery in its Consistory, appropriate enough to the Swiss city-states but destined in different political circumstances to provoke a quite unmedieval separation of Church and State. In all three systems, however—and this is the revolutionary point—we must now look to the layman for action; it is henceforth more than ever impossible to judge the social action of the Church by its ministers. In England, for instance, Council or Parliament must shoulder the main responsibility for Christian action in social and economic affairs, so far as they come within the scope of legislation, while, short of legislation, it is to the layman that we must look for the ' social benefits ' of Christianity. Hooker's affirmation that parliament is not 'so merely temporal as if it might meddle with nothing but only leather and wool' is echoed by Archbishop Tait in 1877: 'If we once get into the way of speaking as if the secular authorities of the land were merely secular, as if their great and only business in Parliament were to make this a rich nation—a nation in which the outward symbols of wealth were to be seen on every side—then, I fear, we might come to a very low style of statesmanship.'[4]

Hooker thought it proper for the State to profit by 'eminent civil ability in ecclesiastical persons'. But the more the emphasis is laid upon the Christian duties of prince and parliament, the more thoroughly can the clergy devote themselves to their own work, the pastoral care of their flocks and the ministry of the Word and Sacraments. For it is predominantly by preaching, writing and informal counselling that the 'official' Church now 'intervenes'. What they said must be considered later on; enough for the moment to note the spate of sermons preached in Tudor England before the King's Majesty, the public sermons at Paul's Cross, the sermons to the nobility and the judges, made more influential by the printing-press. Sermons and published treatises seemed now to be the proper methods of Christian persuasion.

For a time, it is true, the older ecclesiastical courts continued in England. Their right to matrimonial and testamentary jurisdiction was acknowledged, and archdeacons were still busy in their own courts, sentencing scolds and blasphemers and fornicators with spiritual penalties. Archidiaconal correction was resented and increasingly disregarded, while the common lawyers did their best to reduce the area of ecclesiastical jurisdiction, a design in which they were assisted by prevailing uncertainty as to the authority and extent of canon law, since the work of the commission appointed by Henry VIII to formulate a new code had not come to fruition. The older tradition was also at work through two special courts which achieved an unhappy fame in the seventeenth century. The Court of High Commission

was set up to exercise the jurisdiction which had been transferred from the Pope to the Crown by the Act of Supremacy
of 1534; the Court of Star Chamber was a secular court used
to supplement the common law courts by dealing with offences
against statute law, and to enforce royal proclamations. Both
were decidedly royalist and the bishops were strongly represented in them both.

Perhaps the last attempt to mould society by the old ways
and on the old theories was made by Archbishop Laud. In
his time Hooker's constitutionalism had given place to the
divine right of kings, but Laud shared his theory of the one
society of which Church and State are aspects. 'The same
men which in a temporal respect make the Commonwealth
do in a spiritual make the Church.' In the first instance Laud
looked to the ordinary teaching function of the Church to
make good citizens. 'No laws can be binding if there be no
conscience to obey them; penalty alone could never, can never,
do it. And no school can teach conscience but the Church
of Christ.' Much action, however, falls to the State. 'God
will not bless the State if kings and magistrates do not execute
judgement, if the widow and the fatherless have cause to cry
out against the thrones of justice.' And the bishop, Laud believed, must keep king and magistrate up to the mark. 'A
bishop may preach the Gospel more publicly and to far greater
edification in a court of judicature, or at a council-table, where
great men are met together to draw things to an issue, than
many preachers in their several charges can.'[5]

Laud could be wise and foolish, generous and petty. He
had a lofty sense of the priority of public good over private
interest; his outspoken attacks upon wealthy and powerful men
earned him many enemies; and there is a case, at least, for
many of the social measures which he sponsored. In the words
of a biographer quite unsympathetic to Laud's religion, 'The
partnership of the Church and the poor in opposition to
acquisitive landlords was continually being demonstrated, and
Laud, in defending one, was defending the other.'[6] Perhaps
if Parliament had been sitting from 1629 to 1640, his energies

would have been more wisely directed. As it was, he was acting through the unpopular prerogative courts, he fell back after
all on the ' penalties which can never do it ', his intolerance
in Church affairs blinded good men to his constructive social
policy, and he was broken by the rising individualism of his
age.

Liberty

That Christianity is the root of liberty has been as passion-
ately denied as it has been affirmed. Of course, there are
many forms of liberty and many sources of whatever freedom
men have enjoyed. Some are unquestionably secular or non-
Christian. The Athenian ideal of versatile self-fulfilment, revived by the Renaissance, had some share in the making of
nineteenth-century individualism (did not Mill read Homer in
his play-pen?) and was caricatured, with a boost from the new
psychology, in the catchwords of the 1920's. Stoic interest in
the law of nature, though first expressed in terms of duty,
reappears *via* Roman law and some Christian thought in the
natural rights of Locke (who owed much to Hooker), Rousseau
and the political theorists of the American and French Revolu-
tions. In England many of our liberties were won by the
common lawyers who attacked the use or abuse of the royal
prerogative, while for others we are indebted to a purely
political demand, first from the middle and later from the
working classes, for a share in government.

None the less, Christianity has been a force making for freedom. The tyranny which Churches have too often exercised
has always been contrary to two fundamental Christian principles, namely that in conduct every man must stand by his
conscience, and that the supreme fact of life is the relation between God and the individual soul.

The medieval Church, despite its inexcusable methods of
coercion, was also able to protect its members from many
secular tyrannies, since it had established its own corporate
rights over against the State. The Reformers fought against
Rome for religious freedom. Even if they submitted to the

new bondage of the absolute state or the infallible book (and neither is true without qualification) their appeal to the priesthood of all believers, to individual conscience, individual faith, individual use of the Bible, bred a type of man who was soon demanding political and other freedoms. Besides this, the place given to the Protestant layman in the work and government of his own Church has trained successive generations in the methods and principles of democracy, a fact to which the British Labour movement can testify. 'It is probable that democracy owes more to Nonconformity than to any other single movement,' said R. H. Tawney.

In the sixteenth and seventeenth centuries, movements for political and religious liberty went hand in hand. Perhaps politics, more than religion, determined the *opposition* to the Huguenots, who threatened the unity of France; but the Huguenots themselves, though some of their leaders were embroiled in personal and party strife irrelevant to the religious issue, were fighting for freedom of worship. The Dutch revolt flared up in 1567, just after Philip of Spain had ordered that the decrees of the Council of Trent should be enforced in the Netherlands. That it had a political and nationalist aspect is manifest, but its success against the military power of Spain was due to the passionate convictions of Dutch Protestants. These two struggles show how little Calvinists submitted to State absolutism when it threatened their faith. Difficult though it was to lay down a theoretical limit beyond which passive obedience to the ungodly prince is sin, facts would show where the limit had been reached. As Luther had written to Henry VIII, 'Custom, he says, has the force of law. I answer, let it have the force of law in civil causes, but we have been called to liberty, which neither can nor should be burdened with law or custom when we are acting in spiritual causes.'

In England the Elizabethan policy of a single established Church, comprehending variety of thought on the basis of outward uniformity and loyalty to the Crown, came up against Puritan and Presbyterian elements which it could not digest and which eventually broke away to form dissenting churches. With the consequent hardening of Anglicanism, the Independents took up the struggle for liberty, first religious and secondly political. Holland was their nurse and their inspiration. In 1582 Robert Brown wrote from Middelburg a defence of religious liberty which totally repudiated the ecclesiastical authority of the magistrate. In 1593 the exiled Independents fled from London to Amsterdam, to which they were soon followed by congregations from Gainsborough and Scrooby, Lincs. From the Scrooby group, which migrated to Leiden in 1609, came the bulk of the Pilgrim Fathers who sailed in the *Mayflower* in search of freedom.

Next came the English Civil War, another inextricable blend of politics and religion. The Presbyterians who dominated the Puritan party at the outset were quite as intolerant as Laud. They abolished the Book of Common Prayer and imposed the Directory in 1645, and would have riveted their whole system upon the country had they remained an unchallenged majority. Although their defiance of the king in the name of parliamentary government was undoubtedly a step towards political liberty, a wider and deeper freedom was forecast in the *Agreement of the People* which emerged from the debates in the Army Council during the controversy between parliament and army in 1647. The Independents demanded biennial parliaments and manhood suffrage, a revolutionary advance in political liberty which they linked with religious freedom, insisting that neither the Book of Common Prayer nor the Presbyterian Covenant should be compulsory. They stood for toleration, on the ground of liberty of conscience. For Milton, too, the foundation of freedom is a religious truth: 'Man is born free in the image of God.'

The *Agreement of the People* proposed a national religion with its teachers maintained out of the public treasury. But there was to be no compulsion to conform; Christians who differed from it 'shall be protected in the profession of their faith and exercise of religion according to their consciences'. So far, so good. 'Nevertheless it is not intended to be hereby provided that this liberty shall necessarily extend to popery or prelacy.' Though Presbyterianism was established, the *Engagement Act* of 1650 relieved Independents of the obligation to subscribe to the Covenant, and the *Instrument of Government* (1653) followed the religious policy of the *Agreement*, once more refusing to extend liberty to popery or prelacy. Indeed in 1655 Cromwell imposed fresh restrictions upon the episcopalian clergy. Meanwhile certain Anglican theologians — Hales, Chillingworth and Jeremy Taylor — were teaching complete toleration, extending from papist to anabaptist and even to the unbeliever.

What was the outcome of all this? In France the Wars of Religion gave birth to toleration as the only way to prevent national exhaustion. Conceded for this utilitarian reason rather than as a matter of principle, it had nevertheless been won by fidelity to religious conviction. Holland, despite some intolerant blemishes, became a school of many liberties. In England the Independent intolerance of prelacy held up the movement which in other ways they had inspired. The Restoration Church hit back, failing in wisdom and charity, but from 1689 onwards toleration was quickly secured, except by Roman Catholics; and they, while not legally protected, were tolerated in practice. Equality, social and political, took a century longer.

The victory of toleration was not won without cost. The bar to it had not been some devilish spite, but an honest and widespread conviction that the State cannot be religiously indifferent, that an established Church is the condition of national unity, and that Church and State must work together, in one society, to promote Christian morality. Consequently, refusal to conform to the established Church had the air of political and social disaffection. In Elizabethan England, for example, the allegiance of Roman Catholics to the Pope, loyal as they mostly were in fact, aroused just the same suspicion as is evident to-day when Communists are being debarred from certain civil functions because of their allegiance to a foreign power. Religious minorities were the first to teach the State that there are realms over which it cannot be absolute. The right of free association thus vindicated has been a main bulwark against totalitarianism—and its first victim. Unfortunately, it has commonly involved or allowed a secularization of the State. While Calvinism in Geneva could for a time bend the city fathers to its will, minority Presbyterianism in England, unable to get its way through the State, divorced Church from State by its championship of the 'Crown Rights of the Redeemer'. If the State must not interfere in matters of religion, it cannot easily control social morality. The *Church*, said the Puritans, both Presbyterian and Independent, must exercise moral discipline. They objected to the existing ecclesiastical courts both because they were episcopalian and because they were supported by civil sanctions as part of the establishment; and they also objected to any purely secular control of behaviour.

On the Continent, theories of the secular state were put forward by the French Politiques and by the Jesuits, both suggesting that the State as such is neutral in religion, the former to secure peace for France, the latter, like the Puritans, in order to free their Church from government interference. In England, however, the traditional view expounded by Hooker might have been re-asserted at the Restoration, had the English people not been frightened off by the 'little meddlesome hocus-pocus' Laud and by the Puritan legislation of 1642-1660. So toleration joined hands with anti-clericalism to foster *laissez-faire* individualism. Even Hobbes, whose doctrine of the State subjects the individual to the absolute monarch within the sphere of government, limited that sphere to the maintenance of peace and order. 'As nature ordained the banks not to stay but to guide the course of a stream, so it is against sound policy that there should be more laws than necessarily serve for the good of the magistrate and his subjects.'

In such a climate of opinion, reinforced by economic movements which have now to be considered, it is not surprising, however wrong, that the Established Church of the eighteenth century did little to direct social development by any official or concerted action. The eternal dilemma between authority and freedom has yet to be solved.

Economics

The problems which were set to medieval economic morality by the Mediterranean commerce of Genoa and Venice, the bankers of Florence or the cloth merchants of Flanders, were multiplied tenfold by the discovery of America, the Atlantic trade and the money-market of Antwerp. Was it just to confine business of this scale within the old system of gilds, open markets, fixed wages, the just price and the ban on interest? Must the Church condemn what it was impotent to prevent? Or could it distinguish, in its traditional teaching, what did and what did not apply to the changed situation? In Protestant countries, at any rate, the rejection of the Canon Law made room for a new start.

The now familiar controversy over the connection between capitalism and the Protestant ethic seems to have yielded a few assured results. First, capitalism was flourishing long before the Reformation. Secondly, until late in the seventeenth century, the bulk of social teaching among Lutherans, Calvinists and Anglicans was conservative, almost medieval, and decidedly hostile to any relaxation of social control over individual action. But, thirdly, certain elements in Protestant teaching, particularly about work, luxury and individual responsibility, assisted the growth of large-scale industry and commerce on an individualistic and capitalistic basis, though the emancipation of business methods from morality was clean contrary to its intention.

What the Reformers attacked in monasticism was less the scandal of bad monks than the underlying theory that the monastic vocation is intrinsically superior to secular callings. The very use of the words religious and secular rankled. Every calling, they taught, is sacred; every man must serve God in the state to which he is called; and the fact that he is called to work in the world cannot debar him from the highest Christian life. Thus a fresh point was given to the traditional Christian emphasis upon the duty of work.

Luther's social outlook was conservative. He would have liked to preserve the simple agricultural structure of society, benevolent landlord, hard-working peasant, small local industry. He believed in the just price, called usury an invention of the devil and wanted to ' put a bit in the mouth of the holy company of the Fuggers '.[7] No one could be less capitalistic or less sympathetic to commercial enterprise.

Much has been made of the difference between Luther's static idea of serving God *in vocatione* (in one's calling) and Calvin's *per vocationem* (by means of one's calling). If this distinction has been exaggerated, it cannot be denied that Calvin's attitude to business differed from Luther's and had enormously different consequences. He accepted the new world of highly organized international trade and finance as a legitimate sphere of Christian labour, and one which had to be made and kept Christian. He recognized the impossibility of distinguishing in principle between rent from land or houses and interest on capital put into business. He therefore gave a qualified sanction to ' usury '. Nevertheless, the rules governing interest and the whole of business life were to be determined by Christian moral laws, not by ' economic laws ' or greed.

In a way, Protestants were less puritan than Catholics, for they renounced the ascetic theory according to which celibacy is intrinsically higher than marriage, and poverty than wealth. Calvin was as well aware of the danger of riches as any medieval moralist. But in a period of rapid economic expansion the service of God by zeal in one's calling, the contempt of idleness and glorification of hard work, together with austerity in manners, turned out to be the way to accumulate wealth. Work and thrift heaped up riches which might not be spent in personal luxury. Charity, of course, was commanded and found expression in schools, hospitals and other institutions, now predominantly lay foundations. At this time, however, the scorn of idleness modified the forms of charity.

There was work to be done; what the poor needed (it was thought) was the opportunity to earn a living. Hence capital was devoted to keeping them busy, so that even by the path of benevolence, it was ploughed back into business. The results, as well as the motive, could be excellent, but the strain upon personal integrity was great, and was increased as social control relaxed. By the end of the seventeenth century, partly for reasons indicated in the first two sections of this chapter, it was left to the individual to work out and to practise the morality of his business. His Church, of whatever denomination, offered him little but general moral principles.

A further temptation had to be faced. Whereas Calvin had recognized that wealth is not denied to the ungodly, his followers, culling their maxims rather from the Old Testament than the New, looked on worldly success as the divine reward, and therefore proof, of honest industry and sober living. The scope so offered to hypocrisy is divertingly illustrated throughout the English drama of the seventeenth century. Even so, we should not underestimate the integrity of the average religious business man of the period. Though many failed, business had not yet been handed over to an amoral economic necessity.

The control which the Genevan Consistory at first exercised over business life has been summarized by Tawney from Choisy's detailed study. ' It censures harsh creditors, punishes usurers, engrossers and monopolists, reprimands or fines the merchant who defrauds his clients, the clothmaker whose stuff is an inch too narrow, the dealer who provides short measure of coal, the butcher who sells meat above the rates fixed by authority, the tailor who charges strangers excessive prices, the surgeon who demands an excessive fee for an operation. . . . From the election of Beza in place of Calvin in 1564 to his death in 1605, hardly a year passes without a new demand for legislation from the clergy. . . . Throughout there is a prolonged warfare against the twin evils of extortionate interest and extortionate prices.'[8]   Again ' in 1574 Beza preached a sermon in which he accused members of the Council of having intelligence with speculators who had made a corner in wheat. Throughout 1577 the ministers were reproaching the Council with laxity in administration, and they finally denounced it as the real author of the rise in the prices of bread and wine.'[9] Calvin himself had been energetic on behalf of the poor. He secured the foundation of a hospital and a poor-house and got the silk industry started in Geneva to provide work for the unemployed.[10] He insisted on the literal cleaning-up of the city, originating that tradition of cleanliness which still delights the visitor to Geneva. Moreover, he founded the University of Geneva. Soon afterwards, moved by a not altogether unjustifiable anti-clericalism as well as by material interests, the Council shook itself free from the Consistory. Henceforward, as elsewhere, the Calvinist congregation had to be content with its own internal discipline.

Anglican social theory was more conservative than Calvin's. Latimer, Bishop of Worcester, Jewel, Bishop of Salisbury, Archbishops Grindal and Sandys, and the clergy generally, continued to condemn usury, which was prohibited (except from 1545 to 1552) by statute law until 1571, when interest up to ten per cent became lawful. From about that date the officially encouraged popularity of Bullinger's sermons (English Translation, 1577) may have weakened the uncompromising objection to interest. 'Usury,' he wrote, 'is forbidden in the Word of God so far forth as it *biteth* his neighbour.' But ecclesiastical courts still occasionally took action against moneylenders and Anglican moralists long advised against taking interest. Similarly they clung to the just price doctrine and to State price-fixing.

But English theologians of the mid-sixteenth century found agrarian problems more urgent and more perplexing than commercial ones. The main cause was not the transfer of so much land from monastic to lay ownership, but the change from tiny peasant holdings at small rents to large farms at big rents. Landlords now wished to get rid of their customary tenants in order to let their lands on lease at higher rents or with large fines at renewals. Lessees came forward readily

enough, both landlord and tenant-farmer supported the en-
closure of commons, and, with the conversion of arable land
to pasture, the villages were being depopulated.   Again,
ecclesiastical opinion was conservative. The sufferings of the
peasants and the greed of the rich roused the 'Commonwealth's men', led by the layman John Hales and Latimer
the bishop; Archbishop Cranmer, Bishop Scory, Lever, Becon,
Crowley and other prominent divines shared their views and
spoke them out in high places. This group won a notable
short-term victory when the Protector Somerset adopted their
programme. In 1548 he appointed a fact-finding commission,
with Hales as its leader, after which Hales introduced into
Parliament various bills for maintaining tillage, rebuilding
cottages and checking the growth of sheep-farms. Parliament,
however, which naturally represented the landed gentry and
not the peasants, rejected all his most important measures.
Immediately the peasants rose. Warwick won the favour of
the landed classes by his suppression of the curiously mild
and orderly 'revolt' of Kett in Norfolk, Somerset's championship of the poor brought about his fall, and while he was
safely in the Tower, Parliament declared the enclosures to
be legal.

This piece of clerical interference is instructive. Those who
supported Hales displayed courage and true sympathy with
the oppressed. They failed, however, to see the whole picture.
While they vindicated the principle of moral authority in
economics, they did not allow for strictly economic factors.
The fall in the value of money, due to the influx of American
silver and to Henry VIII's debasement of the coinage, made
it unjust that customary tenants should continue to pay a negligible rent and simultaneously receive two or three times as
much for all their produce, leaving the landlord to bear the
brunt of soaring prices. Hales recognized this, but the
admission would have taken the edge off many a sermon.
Further, enclosures often improved farming, and Latimer's
fears for the yeoman were partly falsified by their subsequent
prosperity. It is understandable if the landowners suspected

that the clergy were working off conventional sermons on human greed or bidding for the favours of the poor, or simply making an exhibition of themselves by interfering in something that they did not understand.

Nevertheless, there was enough truth in the Church's case to keep it alive until the Civil War. In a mercantilist system, Tudor and Stuart governments were expected to regulate trade, and could do so the more easily as most foreign trade was in the hands of the big merchant companies while at home many industries were worked under monopolies granted by the Crown. But all such direction had a strictly economic purpose. Laud, by contrast, tried to manipulate the central controls for a moral end, the subordination of private gain to the common good. Social solidarity was his goal, and since the rich could look after themselves, his intention was to protect the poor by an alliance between Church and King. 'I am a great hater of depopulations in any kind, as being one of the greatest mischiefs in this kingdom,' Laud wrote to the Warden of All Souls, Gilbert Sheldon, himself to be one day Archbishop of Canterbury; and when he was impeached in 1644 'Mr. Talbot upon oath deposed how the Archbishop did oppose the law in the business of inclosures and depopulations'.[11] Under Laud's direction Commissions were set up to deal with enclosures and to fix fair wages for craftsmen, the Privy Council busied itself with the food supply, price control and poor relief, and wealthy offenders were heavily fined in the Court of Star Chamber. Reviewing the poor-law policy of the Commonwealth and Protectorate, Godfrey Davies declares that it 'contrasts very unfavourably with the improvement effected by Charles I and the privy council between 1629 and 1640'.[12] Laud, then, must be given his due. No doubt his economic insight was insufficient to solve the problems that faced him, and, as with Somerset and the Commonwealth's men, not all the opposition sprang from greed. His own faults were many. Still, in view of the persistency with which he tried to realize a moral ideal, founded upon religious principles, of the mutual interdependence of all classes, it can scarcely be said that the official Church was doing nothing about society.

Although Puritanism came to prefer ecclesiastical discipline to legislation and eventually fostered individualism and economic freedom, this was no freedom from morality, as the writings of Ames and Baxter sufficiently demonstrate. And during their one spell of political authority they set themselves eagerly to impose their moral ideals upon the country.[13] Adultery was made a crime punishable by death—but juries would not convict. Anti-duelling legislation was severe and fairly successful, being supported by public opinion. From 1655 England saw major-generals suppressing unnecessary ale-houses. Swearing was fined, the Sabbath protected by rigorous rules, rigorously enforced; old sumptuary laws were revived, theatres closed, bear-baiting and cock-fighting stopped. It will be noticed that this legislation differs from Laud's policy in that it is an imposition by law of a number of particular moral precepts, and not of a theory of society. Much of the legislation was beneficial, and still more of its objects were good, though unsuitable for legislation. But the dragooning was too much for the Englishman's taste for liberty. Laud and the Puritans between them created such a dislike of ecclesiastical or governmental interference that the Church of the eighteenth century could do little but preach.

V

The Eighteenth and Nineteenth Centuries in England

'IT is a common error to regard the eighteenth century in England as irreligious. An ethical code based on Christian doctrine was a rule of life to a much larger proportion of the community than it had been in the late medieval and Tudor periods.'[1] 'If, as is the case, the Englishman wherever he is placed, carried with him a sense of duty, this is due to Tillotsonianism.'[2]

'The present age, though not likely to shine hereafter among the most splendid periods of history, has yet given examples of charity, which may be very properly commended to imitation.' (Dr. Johnson in 1758.)

These dicta, if true, go some way towards alleviating the gloom with which Overton and Relton open their history of the Church of England in the eighteenth century: 'It is true that a lover of the English Church cannot study it without a blush. It is a period of lethargy instead of activity, of worldliness instead of spirituality, of self-seeking instead of self-denial, of grossness instead of refinement. There was a grovelling instead of a noble conception of the nature and function of the Church as a Christian society.' True, they go on to sketch in the other side of the picture; and the work of Professor Norman Sykes[3] and others has yet more substantially mitigated the harsh verdicts which were customary. But only mitigated them. The purpose of the following paragraphs is not to exculpate but to understand.

The individualism, tolerance and love of liberty which we prize in English life had gained ground rapidly in the eighteenth century. As Trevelyan writes, 'Reform was to be the specific work of the nineteenth century. The specific work of the earlier Hanoverian epoch was the establishment of the rule of law; and that law, with all its grave faults, was at least a law of freedom. On that solid foundation all our subsequent reforms were built. If the eighteenth century had not established the law of freedom, the nineteenth century in England would have proceeded by revolutionary violence, instead of by Parliamentary modification of the law.'[4] Remembering Charles I and Cromwell, men wanted the minimum of governmental interference with their daily lives. When George III asserted himself, the House of Commons passed the resolution that 'the power of the Crown has increased, is increasing, and ought to be diminished'. Poor relief, for instance, which in the sixteenth, seventeenth and nineteenth centuries was a matter for the central government, was left to the individual justices and parishes. Absolute right in private property was held to be a bulwark of freedom, and in the latter part of the century the domination of Political Arithmetic and *laissez-faire* was complete. As the individualistic theory of property associated with Locke and the main principles of *laissez-faire* were contrary to the main stream of Christian economic doctrine, the Church ought certainly to have made a stand. But it was disarmed by excessive respect for individual responsibility, Christian as that is in its right proportion to social responsibility. There were other influences, too, which worked against vigorous ecclesiastical action.

First, Convocation was silenced from 1717 to 1852. Besides holding up ecclesiastical reform, this hindered (though it should not have been allowed to prevent) the corporate expression of the mind of the Church. For example, the business which would have been before it in 1717 included a protest against duelling. Secondly, the Church was inwardly divided by secular party politics. It had suffered a grave loss by the secession of the Non-Jurors. Subsequently the bishops were mostly Whigs, appointed by Whig governments which were unlikely to restore the Laudian social ethic, while the clergy were mostly Tories, appointed by Tory squires. Thirdly, the poverty of most clergy—now commonly Quiverfuls[5]—tempted them to pay court to the landed gentry or to the government who between them held most of the patronage. The prevailing theory of property, together with the suppression of Convocation, rendered a redistribution of ecclesiastical endowments impossible, as Dr. Johnson explained to Boswell. 'Different men have founded different churches; and some are better endowed, some worse. The State cannot interfere and make an equal division of what has been particularly appropriated.'

These hindrances were demoralizing. It was not simply that the Church took no energetic social action, but that the clergy missed the stimulus which would have come from a public opinion which expected such action. Many were excellent in a restricted field, many were slothful. But they were not often immoral;[6] and there was sense in Bishop Butler's charge to the Clergy of Durham (1751): 'It is cruel usage we often meet with, in being censured for not doing what we cannot do, without, what we cannot have, the concurrence of our censurers.' It would be wrong to leave the impression that the bishops abrogated all social responsibility. When George I showed signs of patronizing the vicious public masquerades, Edmund Gibson, Bishop of London, organized an episcopal petition in response to which the king proclaimed that they should cease after the six already subscribed for. When he went back on his proclamation, sixteen bishops met to plan another attack. Despite Gibson's persistence, court influence was too strong for them, so that they were thrown back after all on preaching. The Church also attacked the appalling outburst of gin-drinking, familiar to us through Hogarth's *Gin Lane*. Secker, later Archbishop of Canterbury, was 'foremost in opposing the Spirituous Liquor Bill of 1743'.[7] These instances are not adduced to suggest that episcopal action was adequate, but to protest against the critics who sweepingly affirm that the Church did nothing.

In theology and in ethical theory alike, benevolence was the keynote of this age. With all his attachment to the rights of private property and his opposition to interference with his business, the Puritan had a strong sense of stewardship. In the eighteenth century this spirit was encouraged among churchmen by the plain moral sermons of Tillotson and the countless preachers who took him for a model. Dr. Johnson's claim was not exaggerated. The important thing about eighteenth century charity is that it was *organized* to avoid mendicancy and to cope with situations which baffled the existing methods of poor relief. Space forbids more than a sample of these foundations.[8] In London, for instance, there were the Westminster Hospital (1719), Guy's (1723), St. George's (1734), the Foundling (1739), the London (1740), the Middlesex (1745), the Lock (1746), the Lying-in Hospital (1749), the City of London (1750), Queen Charlotte's (1752), the Royal Maternity (1757), the Westminster Lying-in Hospital (1765). There was the Marine Society for indigent lads (1756), the Magdalen House (1758), the Thatched House Society (for debtors, 1772). Jonas Hanway was busy with apprentices, workhouses and temperance, General Oglethorpe and John Howard with prisons. These voluntary institutions were not direct Church foundations. Captain Coram indeed met with ecclesiastical opposition to the Foundling Hospital. But, on the whole, they were the direct result of Christian tradition, maintained by Christian preaching. The Hammonds, who will not be suspected of sparing the clergy, write in *Johnson's England*: ' A glance merely at the extracts quoted in this chapter would show how many a parson and magistrate spent his days debating remedies and denouncing wrongs.'[9]

Still more important were the Charity Schools, for England lacked a national system of elementary education, and apart from the little Dames' Schools, the need was met by voluntary foundations and by the Churches. The Charity Schools, in which the Society for Promoting Christian Knowledge played the largest part, spread rapidly through England and Wales. By the end of George I's reign, they existed in every county and numbered some 30,000 pupils. According to their historian 'thousands of schools were set up and hundreds of thousands of children, for whom no other means of education existed, were instructed by its means'. Again, 'It would be difficult to exaggerate the importance and effect of the Charity School movement upon the history and character of the Welsh people.'[10] The schools were free, and open to both boys and girls from the age of seven to twelve. Together with the religious instruction which their promoters desired, reading, writing and arithmetic were taught. Next came the Sunday Schools, which caught on so quickly from about 1780, and which actually contained more scholars than the day schools throughout the nineteenth century. Their object was, of course, religious, but instruction was also given in reading. It is easy to criticize the limitations of Charity and Sunday Schools, both in outlook and technique. But the work was done, thanks to the Churches.

The Church and the Industrial Revolution

When the philanthropic manifestations of Tillotsonian practical Christianity are criticized—and justly—for their failure to challenge contemporary society more radically, it is not always perceived that the defect lay not in its humanitarianism but in its theology. The remedy was not less Christianity, but more. The fierceness with which fundamental doctrines had been debated in the preceding century, causing so much schism and dissension, led by reaction to concentration upon simple moral instruction. Christians seemed at times almost to be afraid of the Holy Spirit. There was not enough either of the passion of the Gospel of Redemption or of the sense of the Church as the Body of Christ bringing the whole created order as an offering to its Lord, to evoke healthy social doctrine. Archbishop Secker, himself long a preacher of Tillotson's school, had recognized this when he charged his clergy to teach the principles not only of virtue and natural religion, but of the Gospel. 'The truth, I fear, is that many if not most of us have dwelt too little on these doctrines in our sermons; by no means, I believe, as disbelieving or slighting them, but partly from knowing that formerly they had been inculcated beyond their proportion and even to the disparagement of Christian obedience, partly from fancying them so generally received and remembered that little needs to be said but on social obligations.' Methodism, the Evangelical Revival and the Oxford Movement had each its part to play before the Church was ready to think constructively about a Christian society.

To be told that Methodism saved England infuriates the 'rationalist'. Listen to one of them. 'Wesley prepared to dedicate his life "to the service of Christ", as he termed his obsession. . . . His influence over peasants and workers was as great as it was baneful. Under his guidance they were lured into the Industrial Age without being aware of what was taking place. . . . Narrow-minded, intolerant, avid of power, ignorant of history or philosophy and indifferent to beauty and the other graces of life, he was the perfect reactionary.'[11] The charges against the Evangelicals, both Wesleyan and Anglican, are that they cared more for people's souls than for their bodies, and that they taught the poor to be content with their lot. To the Christian, the first charge, so stated, needs no defence, whilst those who disbelieve in the soul can hear no defence. It would be quite unfair to the Methodists to say that they did not care about men's bodies, but, even if it were true, it was *someone's* duty to care for souls. The Methodists nobly took up this duty when the parochial system of the Established Church had been completely upset by the growth and rapid shifts of population. The second charge, if moderately stated, contains much truth; the theme of submission to an existing social order was shockingly overworked. Even so, it was and is true that spiritual goods can be possessed by those who lack material goods. The Evangelicals took spiritual wealth to the industrial poor *before* their material poverty could be remedied. Where they failed was not so much in what they taught to the poor as in the substitution of yet more charity for true social reform.

Their positive work was good in the main. Thousands of industrial workers were given the interest in life which their employers denied them, and a moral sobriety for which teachers and taught deserve our gratitude. In the greatest history of England in the early nineteenth century, Halévy writes: 'During the nineteenth century, evangelical religion was the moral cement of English society. It was the influence of the Evangelicals which invested the British aristocracy with an almost Stoic dignity, restrained the plutocrats who had newly risen from the masses from vulgar ostentation and debauchery, and placed over the proletariat a select body of workmen enamoured of virtue and capable of self-restraint.'[12] The Hammonds, too, may be cited: 'There were thousands of men and women in Manchester and Leeds who found self-respect and contentment in the duties and the dreams of their religion. In this way religion made numbers of men and women happier, more unselfish, more ready to undertake burdens for their relief. The Methodist movement did for eighteenth-century England what Christianity did for the ancient world, giving to men of conscience and compassion a cause for which to live, and blending the idea of the brotherhood of man with the most sublime of the mysteries of religion.'[13]

Why then did the Churches not throw themselves into the reform movement? Of course many parsons did, and many reformers were Christian, like Oastler. Lovett, the leading Chartist, was a Methodist, two of the Tolpuddle martyrs, the Loveless brothers, were Wesleyan local preachers, and it was the Vicar of Warwick who led the procession of petition against the Tolpuddle sentences. But the mass of Church opinion, including Nonconformist, was on the other side. Why?

First, a familiar point, the French Revolution set back social progress in England. But for its terrorist leaders and blood-thirsty crowds (doubtless exaggerated in English minds), but for the execution of the king and queen, there would not have been such a fear of the mob, a fear which Evangelicalism made, and Chartism proved, unnecessary, but which was not altogether without justification in big cities before the establishment of a proper police force. Secondly, the intellectual background of the Revolution was anti-Christian, ranging from deism to atheism. Many spokesmen of reform in England belonged to one or other of these schools, so that it was extraordinarily difficult for the Churches corporately to combine with them. The Christian might sympathize with much in Tom Paine's *Rights of Man*, but how could he accept his facile optimism about human nature? or Owen's belief that 'man's character is made for him and not by him'? Similarly Bentham's utilitarianism was a barrier between his reforming efforts and the Churches.

Then there was the tie between social and parliamentary reform. The Church of England, especially in its bishops, was against the latter, wrongly but sincerely, for the bishops could have won an easy popularity by voting for it in the Lords. Early in the century, while, as we tend to forget, England was still mainly agricultural and most of the clergy still lived in the country, the Church wanted to protect agriculture and feared concessions to the manufacturing interest. It could not line up with the Benthamite prophets of industrial progress. Similarly, a little later, Parson Bull of Brierley, near Bradford, the staunchest of social reformers, refused to take part in a demonstration against the Poor Law because it was combined with a demand for universal suffrage.

Sheer ignorance of industrial conditions was one cause, though insufficient excuse, of the slowness with which the clergy turned to reform. For they did turn. As will be seen, a new period began in the Forties after the publication of the great Reports (Epidemics, 1838; Sanitary, 1842; Health of Towns, 1844 and 1845). To this failure in imagination, with which may be compared our own failure to picture to ourselves conditions in China or Central Europe, must be added an intellectual failure for which the country at large, and not the Church, must be held responsible. The rapid growth of population and industry was so bewildering that solutions to many problems were not found till after the damage had been done. Sanitation is an instance. Its importance was not understood, and for some time the authorities could not think how to dispose of refuse in the crowded cities. To those who look back, human blindness is always inexplicable. To take an example outside the scope of religion, the purchase of army commissions was a hindrance to efficiency. Yet ' the system was supported by Wellington, Raglan, and Panmure as late as 1850, and by military opinion as a whole even twenty years later. Palmerston accepted it, and Russell opposed its abolition in 1871.'[14]

Other troubles were due to the absence of central control. There was no law to prevent the speculative builder crowding as many bad small houses as he could into an acre of land; and the small men were worse offenders than the big employers or landowners. For a generation or two, few could throw off the weight of opinion against interference. Liberal in politics, a Christian and future Archbishop, Whately could write as Professor of Political Economy, ' It is curious to observe how, through a wise and beneficent arrangement of Providence, men thus do the greatest service to the public when they are thinking of nothing but their own gain.'[15] The economics of Ricardo and Mill dulled the vision and lulled the consciences of educated men. Freedom had become a fetish and liberty more restrictive than authority.

Police? But a strong police force might subvert liberty. The parliamentary committee of 1818 opined that ' the police of a free country was to be found in rational and humane laws . . . above all in the moral habits and opinions of the people '. Municipal Reform? But the Cambridge Town Council which told the Commissioners that they could do as they pleased with their own property had the law on their side. Schools? It was the radicals who feared to entrust them to the State. ' Education,' Priestley had written in 1768, ' is a branch of civil liberty which ought by no means to be surrendered into the hands of the civil magistrate.' In 1835 Brougham told the Lords, ' It behoves us to take greatest care how we interfere with a system which prospers so well of itself.' Factory Acts? It was again the radicals and liberals, Brougham and Roebuck and so good a man as John Bright, who opposed them. When we sent to the Crimea an army which had scarcely learned to shoot, the War Office could plead the great difficulties of establishing ranges 'in this free country'.[16] 'Centralization. No. Never with my consent. Not English,' said Mr. Podsnap.

So charitable patchwork was preferred to reform. In this the clergy showed initiative as well as energy. Bishop Barring-ton of Durham opened the first Co-operative Distributive Society at Mongewell in 1794. The Rev. J. Smith founded the first Savings Bank at Wendover; the Rev. Henry Duncan estab-lished the first self-sustaining People's Bank in 1810 at Roth-well, a model which eventually led to the Post Office Savings Bank. In 1773 the Rev. James Cowe of Sunbury formed the first philanthropic Friendly Society.[17] The story is continued by the activities of Wilberforce and the Clapham sect and by Shaftesbury's Ragged Schools. Of the 640 London charities in 1862, with an income of some two and a half millions, 279 had been founded between 1800 and 1850.[18] Overlooking the reasons why 'the Churches and sects did not as one man demand social reform from the *Government*', Marjorie Bowen argues that these well-meaning people must have been actuated by love of humanity, not by any religion![19]

Education

The two outstanding achievements of Christianity in this period were elementary education and the abolition of the slave trade. The Charity Schools of the eighteenth century could not reach much of the new population, and the Sunday Schools were educationally inadequate. The ultimate answer, a national system of free and compulsory education, was not arrived at without a great deal of opposition from those who preferred the voluntary system, some in the conviction that education properly belongs to the Church, others out of hos-tility to compulsion and State control as such. Meanwhile the Christian Churches were at work. Their activity was canalized chiefly in two great societies, the Anglican National Society, founded in 1811, and the undenominational British and Foreign School Society (1814) which grew out of the Royal Lancastrian Society (1808). Both adopted the system of teaching by monitors advocated by Dr. Andrew Bell, a clergyman of the established Church, and Joseph Lancaster, a Quaker. The plan was crude, educationally, but effective up to a point; and the schools brought a modicum of instruction to many thousands of children. Indeed it was the vitality of these schools which helped to divert the liberals from the idea of State education. In 1807 Whitbread proposed rate-aid for 'parochial schools under the parochial clergy', as a compromise. He was defeated. In 1820 Brougham introduced an education bill, but dropped it and became an advocate of voluntary schools. For between 1820 and 1834 the number of children in the schools was doubled. A little State aid was granted in 1833—£11,000 for the National Society, £9,000 for the School Society—which was used to build new schools. Unfortunately the Churches damaged their own good gift by denominational disputes, which caused the abandonment of Brougham's Act of 1820 and held up progress in the Thirties. The prospect of considerable State aid could not but cause difficulties about its distribution and the kind of religious education to be given; and public opinion supported the Churches in their rejection of the Radical solution, namely a wholly secular education. By about 1850 the situation had eased, thanks to the conciliatory labours of Kaye-Shuttleworth. Subsequently, however, the sectarian difficulties were kept alive by persistence in the voluntary principle, congenial in itself to the spirit of the age and stiffened by the renewed threat of secularization. The contribution of the Churches to elementary education even after the Act of 1870 is indicated by the fact that out of the million and a half new places for scholars provided from 1870 to 1876, a million were found by them. It may be that in the long run any delay caused by the denominational quarrel was a small price to pay for the vindication of the principle which caused the trouble, that education of the whole person, and not merely of the intellect, must rest upon a religious foundation. We have been spared the divorce between Christian and secular education current in France.

Secondary education also benefited greatly from Christian

founders and headmasters. The public schools were reformed by Arnold of Rugby; Thring of Uppingham showed how to build up the older grammar schools; Woodard founded Lancing and other schools for the middle classes; Marlborough (1843), Rossall (1844) and Radley (1847), among the new public schools, were particularly intended to help the clergy. Durham, first of the modern universities, was founded by the Bishop and the Dean and Chapter of Durham. The improved education of girls was very largely due to Queen's College in London, of which F. D. Maurice was the first principal, and to Miss Buss and Miss Beale, two of its first students, and sturdy Christians. Adult education, stimulated by Brougham, Francis Place and other champions of the working classes, was not specifically Christian in origin, but it was much helped by the Y.M.C.A. (founded 1844) and by Maurice's Working Men's College, which set a higher standard than the mechanics' institutes.

Slavery

Belated as it was, the abolition of slavery and the slave trade in the British Empire was an almost entirely Christian achievement. The attitude of the Church to slavery has received exaggerated praise and exaggerated blame. In its early centuries, Christianity could do little but alleviate the condition of slaves within its own fellowship; it would have been fruitless, and it might have been suicidal, to crusade against the institution itself. The chief boon to the slave, therefore, was the Christian faith, and with it a new personal dignity, compatible with economic indignity because he was treated, equally with the freeman, as a child of God and a brother of every Christian. Several early Popes were slaves; at Carthage in A.D. 203 Perpetua, the lady of good family, and Felicitas, the slave, met death hand-in-hand in the arena.

Humane treatment of slaves was not, of course, peculiar to Christianity. Prudent masters were humane for economic reasons, others, like Pliny, from true goodness. The spiritual equality of all men was taught by Seneca and the Stoics, under whose influence the Antonine emperors passed legislation to improve the slave's lot. It should be observed that this movement did not, any more than Christianity, produce an attack on the institution. Stoicism resembled Christian teaching in insisting on the inward freedom of man, though a slave; and the fact that the admission of so many slaves to the Christian fellowship on an equal footing was brought as a charge against it (by Celsus, for example, in the second century) proves that Christian practice cut deeper than Stoic teaching. Not until the later empire can Christian teaching have affected many slave-owners. At first its contribution lay in rescuing the slaves themselves from the moral degradation which so often accompanies that status. The greatness of this work is untouched by the charge that it was just one more instance of teaching the underdog to be content with his lot.

But when the Church had greater power, it may well be felt that it should have at once attacked the very institution of slavery. Instead, we get more beneficial legislation, particularly from Constantine, Theodosius and Justinian; plenty of moral exhortation to masters and slaves; and much manumission. It is always difficult to understand why one generation perpetuates what a later thinks it should have eradicated. In this case what had been right in the first Christian centuries perhaps became a dead-weight. It was not seen, for instance, that in new circumstances St. Paul's practical instructions needed revision in the light of more fundamental principles in his own theology. Further, Augustine and other leading Christian teachers, who agreed with the Stoics that men are all free by the law of nature, believed that existing social institutions were the result of the Fall. Besides this, the incidence of slavery was changing. Ancient numbers are rarely exact, but the number of slaves in the Greek world and under the Roman republic and early empire was certainly enormous.[20] In the fifth century B.C. a quarter of the inhabitants of Attica had been slaves; Strabo tells us that 10,000 were sold daily in the slave market of Delos (second century B.C.); after the victories of Aemilius

Paulus in Epirus (168 B.C.) 150,000 captives were sold as slaves; Julius Caesar sold 63,000 on one occasion in Gaul; and the number of slaves in the Roman Empire under Claudius (A.D. 41-54) has been calculated as twenty million. By the end of the fourth century, the slave population was so much lower that beneficent legislation and emancipation may well have seemed the way to bring the institution to an end without the difficulties which (as later ages learned) attend a wholesale liberation.

The change was largely economic. The *pax romana* meant fewer captives; the later empire could less afford to keep privileged citizens half idle, and the rigid industrial legislation of Diocletian, by which men were kept working at hereditary trades, together with the development of a rural 'colonate', by which the peasants were tied to the soil but could not be evicted from it, had replaced the large gangs of slave labour with something which, though still very irksome, afforded a measure of economic protection to the poor. It was the surviving domestic slaves who benefited from the emancipation which Christianity encouraged as a work of charity. Far better, no doubt, to have made a clean sweep. But the Christian empire was not based economically on slavery, as had been its predecessors. That, at any rate, had gone.

This movement received a setback—how much, is a matter of controversy—from the barbarian invasions, the wars with the pagan peoples of North and East Europe, and the contacts between Mediterranean Christianity and a slave-owning Islam. Even so, slavery proper was rapidly diminishing in Christian countries. Very little is heard of it in France after about A.D. 1000; according to Domesday Book, there were some 25,000 slaves in England in A.D. 1086. In several other European lands it came near to extinction in the thirteenth century, lingering longest in the eastern Mediterranean and in Portugal. Meanwhile Christian legislation continued, some of the good work of the fourth and fifth centuries having to be done all over again. There were many laws to protect slaves from violence and mutilation, to safeguard their marriages and to prevent the break-up of families. Ethelred II (978-1016) ordered that 'Christian men and uncondemned be not sold out of the country, and especially into a heathen nation, that those souls perish not which Christ bought with His own life'—one among many instances of the effort to prevent Christian bondage to Jews, Moslems and pagans. In the eleventh century Conrad II forbade all traffic in slaves, and Bishop Wulfstan of Worcester successfully fought the slave-trade between Bristol and Ireland. The Council of London (1102) forbade the trade and the Lateran Council of 1179 declared that all Christians ought to be free. It would be easy to multiply examples of what we so often find, action beneficent but tardy and insufficiently drastic. Easy, too, to paint a gloomy picture of surviving abuses. Yet, despite the evil forces of greed and vested interest within the medieval Church, the Christian record was bright in comparison with that of Islam.

The African Slave Trade of recent centuries, if not quite discontinuous with ancient slavery, was a relatively new thing, beginning when both slavery and serfdom were near extinction in many Christian lands. It started in 1442 when the Portuguese explorers of the West African coast were given a present of ten negroes. Thereafter, black slaves were taken to work the Spanish and Portuguese colonies in America. The Bull of Pope Leo X which declared that 'not only the Christian religion but nature herself cried out against the system of slavery' was powerless. It was at this time that one of the noblest of Christians, Bishop Bartolomé de Las Casas, a man who laboured as few have ever done on behalf of exploited natives, made the tragic mistake of which he so bitterly repented. Believing that it would prevent the exhaustion of the native Indians in the mines, he advised that each Spanish resident in Haiti should be allowed to import a dozen negro slaves. Charles V adopted the advice without the limitations and provisions suggested by Las Casas.

England entered the slave trade with Sir John Hawkins in 1562, but the English operations were of no very great size until after the Restoration. In 1713, by the Treaty of Utrecht, England received the contract to supply the Spanish colonies with African slaves; thousands were then shipped every year to Spanish and English possessions. This blot upon our national honour a Christian will not seek to excuse, but he may fairly observe that the traffic was at its worst during the so-called Age of Enlightenment when Christian standards were so much harder to impose. And Christian voices were raised against it as soon as it became prominent. Richard Baxter, the chief Puritan moralist, and George Fox, founder of the Society of Friends, condemned it already in the Restoration epoch. In the next century, the Quakers were pre-eminent in opposition, prohibiting the trade to their own members. Literary men, including Steele, Pope and later Cowper, denounced it; so did Wesley and Whitfield, Dr. Johnson and Bishop Warburton, besides liberal economists like Adam Smith. The theoretical protest thus came from various sources in England, while in France it was voiced by Condorcet and the nationalist philosophers and by Rousseau. Action, however, was principally due, in England, to the combination of the several evangelical groups, Anglican, Methodist and Quaker. In 1772 Granville Sharp, son of a Canon of Durham, secured from Lord Mansfield the famous verdict that a slave who sets foot in the British Islands is *ipso facto* free. The Abolition Society followed, led by Sharp and Clarkson, with Wilberforce as its champion in Parliament. The Clapham sect also founded the Sierra Leone Company, to set up a colony for liberated slaves; Zachary Macaulay, one of the Clapham evangelicals and father of Lord Macaulay, was its first governor. By this time not only the West Indian planters but many a respectable English family was living on an income derived from slave labour. The abolition of the slave trade, which became law in 1807, was a real victory of Christian principle over vested interest. Then, since the abolition of legal trade in slaves made illegal ventures all the more profitable, the next step was the abolition of slavery itself, secured by much the same group of men, reinforced

H

by Thomas Fowell Buxton, in 1833. On 1st August, 1834, the 770,280 slaves of the British Empire became free.

Only the English movement has been included here. It was not an official movement of the Church, but finds its proper place in a book which does not cover the work of individual Christians because it was an organized movement of Christians working together. Whatever praise or blame is due to the Church in the terrible story of slavery, this episode has proved the power of Christian faith and inspiration.

Christian Socialism

The 1840's ushered in a striking change in the social thinking and doing of the Church of England. If the Evangelical Revival and the Oxford Movement diverted many good men from necessary social reform to a one-sided other-worldliness, they had also contributed to the change by their attack upon a life and a society dominated by the pursuit of wealth. Another necessary preparation was the administrative reform of the established Church which took place between 1815 and 1840. Episcopal and capitular revenues were re-distributed, poor livings augmented, churches built in newly populated areas, pluralism and non-residence drastically reduced. The Oxford Movement soon gave rise to higher standards of pastoral responsibility, both diocesan and parochial, and the training of the clergy was improved. So, as E. L. Woodward writes, 'To the average Englishman, and certainly to the average middle-class voter, the legislation of the years 1836-1840 set the Church in sufficiently good order; there were further anomalies to be removed, but, for the time, nothing to cause a scandal.'[21] At about the same time, the clergy were waking up to their social duties. Whereas the first decades of the century found (or made) the working classes bitterly opposed to the established Church, relations between them now improved rapidly. Still conservative in their agricultural policy, and so lukewarm about the Repeal of the Corn Laws (yet the bishops voted 15 to 9 for Repeal), the Anglican clergy were now working energetically for the industrial poor. 'The Vicars of Leeds, Bradford, Wakefield, Huddersfield, Dewsbury, and of many smaller towns, acted as Chairmen regularly at the meetings for the Ten Hours Bill; another Lancashire Vicar, Canon Wray, took the same part at Manchester; the Vicar of Leigh prepared a petition at his own expense. The Church paper, the *Guardian*, gave strong support to the Bill.'[22] A Burnley newspaper was provoked into complaining of the leading part taken by the Church in the 'agitation'. And many working men must have known that the immense labours of Shaftesbury on their behalf were inspired by his religion. Meanwhile the Nonconformist ministers befriended the poor against the landowners, and the democratic government of the Free Churches was training the labour leaders of the future.

One thing was still lacking, a theology of society. How impossible some Christians found co-operation with social reformers of an un-Christian or anti-Christian tendency has already been noticed. But for a time the Church put forward no constructive alternative. The difficulty is made plain by the man who most helped to meet the need, F. D. Maurice. 'Every hope I had for human culture, for the reconciliation of opposing schools, for blessings to mankind, was based on theology. What sympathy then could I have with the Liberal Party, which was emphatically anti-theological, which was ready to tolerate all opinion in theology only because people could know nothing about it, and because other studies were much better pursued without reference to it?' In later life, J. S. Mill recanted a great deal of the theory on which the liberal reforms had been based; the defects were earlier apparent to many Christians, as to Maurice. Although the first Tractarians did not directly provide a Christian sociology, their insistence that there is a specifically Christian life distinct from that of the world (as the Evangelicals were also teaching), that the Church is a spiritual society essentially independent of the State and that the Christian life means Christian fellowship, prepared the way for new social thought.

It did not come from the immediate successors of the Tractarians. Maurice was an independent and comprehensive thinker, influenced by the Oxford Movement, but also by Coleridge, Southey and Carlyle. As he said of himself, he 'felt as a theologian, thought as a theologian, and wrote as a theologian'. 'All other subjects are to my mind connected with theology, and subordinate to it.' It was his task to work out the social implications of the Christian faith, of the Creation, the Incarnation, the Redemption wrought by Christ, the Church and the Sacraments, the unity of men in Christ. Upon this unity, he taught, society must be built. Hence his Christian Socialism, which meant primarily the association of workers in the control of and responsibility for production, as against the principles represented by the words 'hands' and 'competition'. 'I hold that there has been a sound Christianity in the world, and that it has been the power which has kept society from the dissolution with which the competitive principle has been perpetually threatening it.'

The practical men of the movement, Charles Kingsley, Tom Hughes, J. M. Ludlow and E. V. Neale, all looked upon Maurice as their master, for all were fired by his ideal of Christian community. Kingsley caught the popular ear with his letters of Parson Lot in *Politics for the People* (1848) and his novels *Yeast* (1848) and *Alton Locke* (1850); later his *Water Babies* (1863) helped Shaftesbury's fight for the boy chimney-sweeps. Besides his writing, Kingsley threw himself with immense vigour into the cause of sanitary reform. Ludlow, Neale and Hughes tried to make the principle of association effective in co-operative societies. The co-operative movement, which we saw in embryo at Mongewell (p. 107), sprang mainly from Robert Owen. On its consumer or distributive side, the right pattern was found by a group of Chartist and Owenite workmen, the *Rochdale Pioneers*, in 1844. It had already attracted Christian support, notably from a theologically-minded physician, Dr. William King of Brighton, who edited its monthly magazine, *The Co-operator*, from 1828 to 1830. A generation later, Neale and Hughes were outstanding among its leaders, side by side with the secularist Holyoake. Ludlow, who had first-hand knowledge of French socialism, was more interested in co-operative production. His first foundation was the Tailors' Association of 1850, just after Kingsley's denunciation of sweating and the current political economy in *Cheap Clothes and Nasty*. Associations for builders, cobblers, bakers, smiths, piano-makers and needlewomen followed. This form of guild socialism was intended to show, according to Ludlow, 'how working men can release themselves from the thraldom of individual labour under the competitive system; or at least how far they can at present by honest fellowship mitigate its evils'. The first associations had a hard struggle and were not very successful. They were in themselves only a tiny contribution to the general working-class movement, while trades unions received more useful support from Nonconformity. But the Christian Socialists were foremost in obtaining the Industrial and Providential Societies Act of 1852, the charter of co-operative societies.

Bridges had now been built across the gulf between the Church and the working-classes. In contrast with continental socialism, the British Labour movement grew up within, rather than in opposition to, the Christian tradition, a fact of overwhelming importance in the life of the nation. But the Fifties and Sixties were not propitious to Christian or any other socialism. Individualism and self-help, free trade and *laissez-faire* were in command. For some years it was possible to argue that industrialism had got over its growing pains and was now to shower its bounty upon the whole people; progress seemed inevitable. After 1870, however, in the words of Trevelyan, 'Democracy, bureaucracy, collectivism are all advancing like a silent tide making in by a hundred creeks and inlets.'[23] By now Labour may be politically too strong to bother much whether it has the support of the Churches. But until fairly recent times it was still true, as it had been a century ago, that many a labour leader owed his inspiration and his training to his church or chapel, while the intellectuals of the movement were not infrequently drawn into its service through directly Christian Settlements, such as Toynbee Hall.

It is not to be supposed, however, that the Churches are only doing their social duty when they are fostering labour movements. It would be easy to enumerate particular social services rendered by bishops to the community, from Archbishop Whately's successful campaign against the transportation of convicts to the citizen-bishop Fraser of Manchester[24] and Bishop Westcott's work for the Durham miners; easy, also, to instance some of the laity of the nineteenth century whose great services sprang straight from their Christian faith—Shaftesbury, Florence Nightingale, Josephine Butler, Octavia Hill, for example. But lists of names give no true picture of what Christians have done well or of what they have left undone or done amiss. There is now less danger of the Church being indifferent to society than of society being indifferent to the Church, or of believing that the Church should, after all, keep its religion to itself (for those that like such things!), leaving the State or the people or the intelligentsia to carry on the real business of the world without it. Disastrous as this would be, there is a grain of truth in it so far as concerns the clergy. The State has taken to itself so many activities which once were initiated and maintained by the Church[25] that the ministers of the Church cannot now be held responsible for them; certainly not for their management in detail. Though this trend has robbed the Church of many opportunities, it also makes it possible for the clergy to devote themselves to their most proper work, while the school-teachers bemoan the social duties which have been thrust upon them.

Not that the clergy will give up their contacts with people, retiring to a maximum of pious exercises, but that their work will be evangelistic, pastoral and intellectual, the Ministry of the Word and Sacraments. The last century opened with a great new mass of people growing up as heathen, indoctrinated by their own leaders with hostility to the Church, a mass which had not been lost to Christianity, but never won for it.

Methodists, Evangelicals and the slum-priests of the Oxford Movement began a work which has ever to be renewed in changing circumstances. As the existing parochial system of the late eighteenth century was not ready for the Industrial Revolution, so the methods of church and chapel to-day must be revised, for example by the use of factory and other non-territorial chaplains, without losing what is good in the parochial unit. Pastorally the Christian layman needs help to see the moral and social obligations of his job, his leisure and his citizenship. Intellectually, he must be given a Christian view of life as a whole and taught how to defend it among his fellows. Whatever its failures, the Church of the nineteenth century thought its way through the intellectual challenge of the theory of evolution and its application to historical scholarship. Moreover, in the line of theologians that runs from Maurice through Westcott, Scott Holland and Gore to William Temple, the Church of England set about the task of working out the Christian basis of modern society. For though it is too much to suppose that the Church ought officially to provide an exact pattern of society,[26] it is too little to say that the layman must behave Christianly in his work. What is necessary is corporate Christian thinking about the whole life of the community; and this Christians are doing, perhaps as never before. It is by creating a truly Christian and informed public opinion that the Church can fulfil its social duty. It is impossible for the Church to offer its services, as a useful organization, to the secular State on secular terms. The Church stands for God's terms, the dependence of a society upon the will and purpose of its Creator, the dependence of weak, foolish and sinful men upon the grace of Jesus Christ in the fellowship of the Holy Spirit.

The Wider Fellowship

The plan adopted in this book has by this time narrowed our vision to the Churches in England. It must close with a wider vista. How can the world find fellowship in the ways of peace and justice? The last hundred years have seen three

Christian contributions which have yet to bear their fruit. First, the World's Student Christian Federation, comparatively modern, pregnant with possibility. No man can yet estimate what the fellowship of university students of all nations may do for the world. Second, the Ecumenical Movement, the rising tide of Christian unity. Again, no man can tell what results its success would have. Third, and above all, the modern missionary movement. In a century the map of Christianity has been redrawn; where there were little groups of Christians or none at all, there are Christian nations and indigenous churches.[27] All these movements are faced with great difficulties. Humanly speaking, it looks like a race between religion and irreligion, and there are many who would interpret it as a race in which a dying creed is being outrun by the secularism of the future. But the last word is with God. We have spoken of the early Church, the Middle Ages, modern times. Are not these terms getting out of date? Who knows how *young* the Church is?

Authority and Freedom

The problem of authority and freedom confronts us throughout history. For centuries the Church was the accepted authority, with the State, not individual liberty, as the alternative. Emancipation from the authority of the Church has sometimes increased that of the State, and sometimes fostered an individual freedom which seemed to have been won once and for all in Western Europe and America. To-day, however, the conflict between totalitarianism and liberty is more acute than any between Church and State or Church and individual in the past. Whereas in the nineteenth century the Church helped, if tardily, to correct an excessive individualism, a chief social function of Christianity will now be to safeguard the individual. There is much truth in Macneile Dixon's outburst: 'The passion for reforming one's neighbours out of existence, or at least out of the existence they prefer—and the two are often found together—afflicts even more grievously those who have lost their faith in God than those who believe in Him. The seceders to the Church of the ethical idealists, having dispossessed God of His authority, are at no loss to replace Him. They mount the vacant throne, deify their own consciences, would have men bow and worship their ideals, and proceed to establish a tyranny more irksome than that of their ecclesiastical predecessors:

> More haughty and severe in place
> Than Gregory or Boniface.

" Be my brother, or I will slay you." Who conferred upon them this astounding magistracy? '[28]

The Church will not reclaim its old official power, the clergy will not control the machinery of government or dictate their views to docile or resentful lay figures. The tolerance which the State is losing is more secure within a Church which has now learned to work by the persuasion of truth and love. And what authority can be asserted against the State save that of God? For mere individualism has been proved inadequate to protect the weak or to grapple with the complexities of modern society.

Two things are vital. Socially, Christians will promote not so much the old-fashioned charity, though that will always be necessary, as community, genuine partnership in every walk of life, in family, school, factory,[29] government, in the house of God. Spiritually, the Church must preserve its other-worldliness. The very tension which has often perplexed the noblest Christians and hindered social progress is nevertheless essential. For the only answer to the all-devouring State, if it is an evil one, is that its ends are contrary to God's and must be resisted; if it is a ' welfare ' State, that it is only a means to an end, and that the divine purpose to which it must subordinate itself is not to be realized in a historical Utopia, but in the Kingdom of Heaven, in a divine society of individual persons beyond history.

Notes

CHAPTER I

1 Compare M. Bowen, *The Church and Social Progress* (Thinkers Library, 1945), p. 10: ' Most pernicious of all the priests' activities was their zestful work in politics,' with p. 69: ' None of these prelates, pastors, or gospel preachers, led his flock to the Houses of Parliament.'

2 B. J. Kidd, *Documents Illustrative of the History of the Church* (S.P.C.K., 1923), II, nos. 34, 36, 79.

3 Augustine, *Epistles*, 50, 133-4, 90-1, 103-4, 113-16, 189.

4 Kidd, *Documents*, no. 23; and for Ambrose and Theodosius, 109, 110.

CHAPTER II

1 F. Lot, *The End of the Ancient World*, Eng. trans., pp. 386-7.

2 *ib.*, 385.

3 *Epistles*, VI, 12, Eng. trans., O. M. Dalton, II, 94.

4 Gregory of Tours, *History of the Franks*, Eng. trans., I, 267.

5 F. M. Stenton, *Anglo-Saxon England* (Oxford History of England), p. 142.

6 *op. cit.*, I, 264.

7 *Cambridge Mediaeval History*, I, 540.

8 The crossword puzzler may like to have their names: xenodochia, nosocomia, ptochotrophia, brephotrophia, gerontocomia.

9 M. Dobb, *Studies in the Development of Capitalism*, p. 79.

10 Stenton, *op. cit.*, 269.

11 Dalton, *op. cit.*, I, 45 (Clovis); 62 (Chilperic); 56, 52 (Guntram); 75 (Fredegond); 387 (nobles).

12 *ib.*, 242.

CHAPTER III

1 H. Pirenne, *Economic and Social History of Mediaeval Europe,* Eng. trans., I. E. Clegg (London, 1936), p. 13.

2 W. Stubbs, *The Constitutional History of England*[5] (Oxford, 1891), I, 388; cf. 330.

3 *ib.*, I, 380.

4 *ib.*, I, 676; and cf. Powicke in *Cambridge Mediaeval History*, VI, 232, for the importance of Walter and King John's mistakes when free of him.

5 E. F. Jacob in *Cambridge Mediaeval History*, VI, 28.

6 A. L. Smith, *Church and State in the Middle Ages*, p. 51.

7 T. Plucknett, *A Concise History of the Common Law*[3] (Butterworth, 1940), p. 270.

8 R. H. Tawney (*Religion and the Rise of Capitalism*, ch. I, note 88) points out that *Surtees Society*, vol. lxiv (*Ripon Chapter Acts*), ' contains more than 100 cases in which the court deals with questions of contract, debt, etc. '; cf. note 87: ' It seems probable that a more thorough examination of the Early Chancery Proceedings would show that, even in the fifteenth century, the jurisdiction of the ecclesiastical courts in matters of contract and usury was of greater practical importance than has sometimes been supposed.'

9 H. D. Hazeltine in *Cambridge Mediaeval History*, V, 731.

10 For these laws see F. L. Attenborough, *The Laws of the Earliest English Kings* (Cambridge, 1922).

11 F. M. Stenton, *Anglo-Saxon England*, p. 273.

12 Holdsworth, *A History of English Law*, II, 143.

13 Plucknett, *op. cit.*, 614.

14 Cicero, *De Officiis*, I, paras. 34-8, 80, 82.

15 Ambrose, *De Officiis*, I, 36.

16 The founders of modern international law, Albericus Gentilis and Hugo Grotius, had in a sense to untheologize law in order to get any accepted as binding upon States. But their conception of natural law was theologically grounded. Grotius, a Christian theologian, was really trying to bring international relations under moral control, against contemporary ' Machiavellianism '.

17 Gregory, *Registrum*, II, 73.

18 Innocent, *Ep.*, 73.

19 T. S. R. Boase, *Boniface VIII* (Constable, 1933), 145, 204, 206.

20 For these and other instances, not all equally convincing, see J. Eppstein, *The Catholic Tradition of the Law of Nations*, London, 1935.

21 The Manichees believed that matter was not created by God, but is in itself evil and the cause of sin. The loftiest morality, therefore, demands renunciation of all material goods. Theologically this implied the denial of our Lord's full humanity. The Catharists (' pure ones ') revived similar teaching, especially in the South of France (the Albigensians).

22 R. H. Tawney, *Religion and the Rise of Capitalism* (Pelican, 1938), 52.

23 ' Give a loan, expecting nothing back.' The original Greek can be differently explained, as may be seen from a comparison of A.V. and R.V. The interpretation given above, which is almost that of A.V., was the one accepted in the Middle Ages.

24 E. Troeltsch, *The Social Teaching of the Christian Churches*, Eng. trans., Olive Wyon (Allen & Unwin, 1931), I, 320.

25 Holdsworth, *op. cit.*, II, 283.

26 For medieval missions see K. S. Latourette, *A History of the Expansion of Christianity*, Vol. II.

27 Ramon Lull (born at Majorca *c.* 1235, died 1315) was important as poet, mystic and missionary. He learned Arabic, preached to Moslems at Tunis (1291) and Bougie (1304, 1314). He was twice imprisoned and finally stoned to death at Bougie. He proposed the foundation of missionary colleges and the teaching of oriental languages in universities and monasteries. Cf. E. A. Peers, *Fool of Love* (S.C.M. Press, 1946).

Chapter IV

1 R. N. Carew Hunt, *Calvin*, p. 150.

2 Troeltsch's account of Luther's teaching has been severely criticized by subsequent students of Luther, but is often repeated. I am sure that I have not grasped Luther's conception of the place of natural law and the Gospel, and, though I have not followed Troeltsch, I may still have conceded too much to his point of view.

3 Richard Hooker, *Of the Laws of Ecclesiastical Polity*, Book VIII.

4 R. T. Davidson and W. Benham, *Life of A. C. Tait* (Macmillan, 1891), II, 300.

5 For Laud see Tawney, *op. cit.*, 159-62, and H. R. Trevor-Roper, *Archbishop Laud* (Macmillan, 1940).

6 Trevor-Roper, *op. cit.*, 169.

7 A famous German family of merchants and bankers.

8 Tawney, *op. cit.*, 117.

9 *ib.*, 120.

10 Cf. A. Dakin, *Calvinism* (Duckworth, 1940), p. 149.

11 Tawney, *op. cit.*, 279.

12 G. Davies, *The Early Stuarts* (Oxford History of England), p. 298.

13 *ib.*, 301-12.

Chapter V

1 Trevelyan, *English Social History*, p. 353.

2 Baring Gould, quoted by Trevelyan, p. 357.

3 For example, his *Edmund Gibson* and *Church and State in England in the Eighteenth Century*.

4 *English Social History*, p. 351.

5 Take any volume of the *Dictionary of National Biography* (the 1921-1930 supplement will do very well) and you will see the contribution of the *sons* of the clergy to the life of the nation. The proportion is astonishing.

6 See the testimonies collected in Abbey and Overton, *The English Church in the Eighteenth Century*, II, 47-8.

7 *Dictionary of National Biography*, s.v. Secker.

8 I have taken the list partly from *Johnson's England* (Oxford, 1933) and partly from an essay by Professor Norman Sykes in the *Historical Magazine* of the Protestant Episcopal Church of America, Sept. 1947. Consult also J. H. Hutchins, *Jonas Hanway* (S.P.C.K., 1940).

9 *Johnson's England*, p. 329.

10 M. G. Jones, *The Charity School Movement* (Cambridge, 1938), pp. 3 and 321.

11 M. Bowen, *op. cit.*, 50, 52.

12 Quoted by Trevelyan, *op. cit.*, 477.

13 J. L. and B. Hammond, *The Age of the Chartists*, p. 253.

14 E. L. Woodward, *The Age of Reform* (Oxford History of England), p. 258.

15 Quoted in C.O.P.E.C. Report (1924), XII, 134. Compare J. S. Mill, reviewing his earlier opinions in the last chapter of his *Autobiography*: ' In those days I had seen little further than the old school of political economists into the possibilities of fundamental improvement in social arrangements. Private property, as now understood, and inheritance, appeared to me, as to them, the *dernier mot* of legislation: and I looked no further than to mitigating the inequalities consequent on these institutions, by getting rid of primogeniture and entails. The notion that it was possible to go further than this in removing the injustice—for injustice it is, whether admitting of a complete remedy or not—involved in the fact that some are born to riches and the vast majority to poverty, I then reckoned chimerical, and only hoped that by universal education, leading to voluntary restraint on population, the portion of the poor might be made more tolerable.'

16 Woodward, *op. cit.*, 258.

17 C.O.P.E.C., XII, 129.

18 A table is given in *Early Victorian England* (Oxford, 1934), II, 320.

19 *op. cit.*, p. 70.

20 See *Encyclopaedia Britannica*, art. ' Slavery ' for the figures. I do not vouch for them all. The articles on ' Slavery ' in Hastings, *Encylopaedia of Religion and Ethics*, are valuable summaries.

21 *op. cit.*, 492. For details, see W. L. Mathieson, *English Church Reform*, 1815-1840 (Longmans, 1923).

22 Hammond, *op. cit.*, 288.

23 *English Social History*, p. 552.

24 ' He (Fraser) was Bishop of all the denominations and the most potent public man in the district. . . . He was everywhere at once, talking to cabmen, railway workers, theatre folk and cotton workers. . . . His death in October, 1885, was noted by a statue to " Our Bishop ", erected by popular subscription.' (*Bulletin of John Rylands Library*, Jan. 1948, p. 7); cf. Thos. Hughes, Q.C., *James Fraser* (Macmillan, 1887).

25 Youth Clubs are a recent example.

26 There is some division of opinion among Christian sociologists about the limits of Christian planning. See M. Reckitt, *Maurice to Temple* (Faber, 1947), p. 199.

27 See Latourette, *op. cit.*, for detail, and, for an unusual glimpse of little known Christian work, H. P. Van Dusen, *They Found the Church There* (S.C.M. Press, 1945).

28 W. Macneile Dixon, *The Human Situation*, p. 206 (Gifford Lectures, 1937).

29 It has very quickly become clear that collectivist nationalization does not satisfy the worker's just ambition to have a real share in policy and management.

ADDITIONAL NOTE

Extract from a letter from J. M. Keynes to Archbishop Temple in 1941, about the eighteenth century:

" Leaving out the Scots, such as Hume and Adam Smith, and foreign residents in London, such as Mandeville and Cantillon, I can think of no one important in the development of politico-economic ideas, apart from Bentham, who was not a clergyman, and in most cases a high dignitary of the Church. For example, Dean Swift interested himself in these matters. Bishop Fleetwood wrote the first scientific treatise on price and the theory of index numbers. Bishop Berkeley wrote some of the shrewdest essays on these subjects available in his time. Bishop Butler, although primarily of ethical importance, is not to be neglected in this field. Archdeacon Paley is of fundamental importance. The Reverend T. R. Malthus was the greatest economist writing in the eighteenth century after Adam Smith."—Iremonger, *William Temple* (O.U.P., 1948), p. 439.

Temple's own life is an outstanding example of clerical thought and action in social affairs.

Index

(a) Subjects

(b) Names